WESTON M EDWARDS, PH.D.
DAVID DELMONICO, PH.D.
and ELIZABETH GRIFFIN, MA

CYBERSEX UNPLUGGED

FINDING
SEXUAL HEALTH
IN AN
ELECTRONIC
WORLD

A BOOK IN THE
LIVING A LIFE
I LOVE™
SERIES

Copyright Page

Cybersex Unplugged: Finding Sexual Health in an Electronic World.

SERIES: Living a Life I Love™

For additional copies of this workbook, please visit or email:

Weston Edwards, PhD

request@sexualhealthinstitute.org
www.livingalifeilovebooks.com

ISBN 145362645X
EAN-13 9781453626450.

Disclaimer. This information provides accurate and authoritative information regarding sexuality; the information is for education purposes only. The publisher and authors are not engaged in providing professional services. You should seek the services of a trained professional if you need expert assistance or therapy services.

Table of Contents

Introduction

Stories from the net.

"Frank," says the boss, "we're letting you go. I.T. has been tracking the sites you're visiting on the web while at work. I warned you about this before…"

Molly is shocked when Little Susie talks about the "naked people on the computer."

Richard says, "I'm stunned that my wife was using the Internet to have an affair."

Mom wants Dad to have the birds you – not *and-bees talk with Mikey after she walked in on him masturbating to porn.*

"How did you get a $2200.00 phone bill?"

News Headline, "Child Porn sting nets 17 individuals, including a teacher."

MSNBC Headline, "Pastor caught in 'To Catch a Predator.'"

Recent outbreak of Chlamydia linked to Adult Sex website.

These stories express many of the struggles with the Internet. They express the darker side of the Internet. Unfortunately, they are only the surface of the problem. The stories belie the daily anxiety framed by the following questions:

Does anyone track what I'm doing online?

How do I hide what I'm doing from my partner?

OMG, did she see what I was doing?

I hope the person on the other side is as hot as they say they are.

I get so tired of the online games.

I don't have any real friends.

I'm only online because I can't have sex with my partner.

Boy that chat was great; is that cheating?

It's not cheating if we don't have sex, is it?

Is that pic legal?

This workbook resulted from conversations with individuals who struggle with their online sexual behavior. The consensus from these individuals (and many therapists) was a need for a current workbook addressing the common issues for cybersex compulsivity. This book builds on our experience in sexual compulsivity to focus on the nuances of Internet sexual compulsivity. We break down the complex elements of treating cybersex problems into the basic elements for the individual to address. We also highlight what we think are issues unique to cybersex including topics such as psychology of the Internet, cybersex user categories, and understanding, assessing, and managing your Internet use. The three of us represent over 50 years of clinical and research work. Much of what we write is based on our clinical experiences, research on other related topics helpful in addressing cybersex, and in all honesty a bit of a "guess." We hope you find this workbook useful as you strive to find sexual health in an electronic world.

This workbook focuses on cybersex; as such it is limited to cybersex. We believe cybersex is a subset of a larger field of sexual compulsivity. This workbook is not meant to address the larger topic of classic sexual compulsivity that is broad, with a variety of factors and addressed in the first book by Dr. Edwards, *Living a Life I Love*. This workbook also contains material adapted from Dr. Delmonico and Ms. Griffin's previous book (co-written with Dr. Patrick Carnes), *Cybersex Unhooked* which is out of print but available for download at www.Internetbehavior.com.

What Is In a Name?

Although the focus of this book is problematic online sexual behavior, it is important to understand the broader issue of problematic sexual behavior. When it comes to the field of problematic sexual behavior, coming up with a blanket definition and universal term is a challenge. Previous and current terms to describe problematic sexual behavior have been widely misused or overused and include "sexual compulsivity," "sexual compulsion," "sexual addiction," "sexual impulsivity," "sexual obsession," "sexual anorexia," "out-of-control sexual behavior," "sexaholism" and, finally, but certainly not the most obscure, "love addiction." Newer research focuses on the term "hyper-sexuality" but this term misses the struggle of those who avoid sex.

The term "cybersex" has become a catchall to describe a variety of computer based sex related behaviors. These behaviors can include accessing online pornography (audio, video, text), engaging in sexual chat with others, creating an avatar to engage in sexual acts or chat, using sex toys designed for the online world, or a combination of all the above. In no way are we able to describe and address all cybersex behaviors. More variations of online behavior are being developed as the Internet changes on a daily basis.

As a field, there is a range of accepted opinions of what term to use. Generally, in this book we prefer the term sexual compulsivity in describing out of control offline sexual behaviors and cybersex compulsivity in describing out of control online sexual behavior.

When Does Cybersex Become Compulsivity?

It is important to understand that not everyone who engages in cybersex behavior has a problem with compulsivity. Research indicates about 85% of individuals who engage in cybersex behaviors do so without serious consequences.

In thinking about your cybersex behavior and determining whether it is problematic or out of control in your life, there are two components.

Subjective – Realization that a Problem Exists

On some level you recognize your online sexual behavior is a problem. Cybersex compulsivity includes many sexual behaviors or thoughts that violate your personal values and boundaries. These behaviors often lead to feelings of guilt, shame, and self-recrimination. In psychology, we call this "ego-dystonic:" "I know I did something I didn't want to do." The vast majority of people seeking help realize they need help. The key to treatment, however, requires additional information as to why, what, who, when and where the problem lies. This is the focus of the workbook.

Objective – External Notification of a Problem

You may not have realized there is a problem, but some form of external feedback has presented itself to bring the situation to light. This feedback can come in the form of a legal consequence (such as an arrest), a financial consequence (such as money spent on the Internet, or termination from a job) or damage to a relationship because of the violation of boundaries. For some people, the objective component of sexual compulsivity may not always be present. An external factor is useful when there is a high level of denial by an individual regarding the impact of the behavior.

What part of your online behavior is compulsive is sometimes hard to define. Often your answer might be, "It depends." The answer will depend on the presence of consequences, your values and your relationship agreements with others (e.g., your marriage/partnership). The basic premise of our approach is that you define healthy and unhealthy behaviors in dialogue with others. At the same time, there are behaviors that automatically raise questions. For example, research suggests that spending 11 or more hours a week viewing Internet pornography is one warning sign of Internet sexual compulsivity. This number, however, does not conclusively determine whether or not your Internet behavior is sexually compulsive. As you go through the workbook, sometimes the same behavior may or may not be compulsive, depending on the day, your mood and other circumstances. It will be most helpful for you to pay attention to whether there is a repetitive and consistent pattern to your behavior, and how the consequences of your behavior may be affecting your life and relationships. As you progress through the workbook, it will become easier to determine whether your cybersex behavior has become problematic or compulsive.

Sexual compulsivity or cybersex compulsivity is not the same as sexual promiscuity. Sexual compulsivity or cybersex compulsivity can occur in the absence of sexual behavior. Examples include obsessive thoughts or fear of sex (sometimes referred to as "sexual anorexia" or "sexual avoidance"). Sexual compulsivity or cybersex compulsivity are also not the same as pedophilia (defined as an attraction to children). While these problems may sometimes overlap, the issues are separate therapeutic concerns.

Creating Sexual Health, Offline and Online

One of the major goals of this workbook is to assist you in clarifying healthy sexual behavior, both offline and online. We believe that in order to be healthy online, sexually or otherwise, you must develop healthy sexuality offline as well. In order to achieve this goal, it is important to understand what sexual health is. We prefer the World Health Organization's 2002 definition that defines sexual health as:

> a state of physical, emotional, mental and social well being related to sexuality; it is not merely the absence of disease, dysfunction or infirmity. Sexual health requires a positive and respectful approach to sexuality and sexual relationships, as well as the possibility of having pleasurable and safe sexual experiences, free of coercion, discrimination and violence. For sexual health to be attained and maintained, the sexual rights of all persons must be respected, protected and fulfilled.

Creating sexual health is more a process than a response to a yes or no question. Our goal is to provide you the tools to help you develop and improve your sexual health both online and offline.

The Ten Components of the Sexual Health Model

To help you move toward sexual health, the topics in this workbook are based on a theoretical model of sexual health that consists of 10 components, which we briefly summarize here.[1] You will be addressing these topics throughout the workbook.

Talking About Sex
This is a cornerstone of the Sexual Health Model that includes talking about one's own sexual values, preferences, attractions, history and behaviors.

Culture, Values and Stereotypes
In order to understand a sense of sexual self, individuals must examine the impact their particular cultural heritage has on their sexual identities, attitudes and behaviors.

Sexual Anatomy and Functioning

One needs a basic understanding, knowledge and acceptance of sexual anatomy, sexual response and sexual functioning. Sexual health includes freedom from sexual dysfunction and other sexual problems.

Sexual Health Care and Safer Sex

There are many components to this, including knowing one's body, administering regular self-exams and responding to physical changes with appropriate medical intervention. Examining one's safer sex behaviors is critical.

Challenges and Barriers to Sexual Health

Some of the major challenges include sexual abuse, substance abuse and compulsive sexual behavior. Others include sex work, harassment and discrimination.

Body Image

This requires challenging the notion of one narrow standard of beauty and encouraging self-acceptance. In order to achieve sexual health one needs to develop a realistic and positive body image.

Masturbation, Fantasy and Sexually Explicit Material

Masturbation and fantasy can each be healthy expressions of sexuality. It is important for individuals to clarify their values on these subjects. Too often, shame is linked with masturbation and fantasy because of the historical myths associated with sin, illness and immaturity.

Positive Sexuality

All human beings need to explore their sexuality in order to develop and nurture who they are within a positive and self-affirming environment. Positive sexuality includes appropriate experimentation, sensuality, sexual boundaries and sexual competence developed through the ability to give and receive sexual pleasure.

Intimacy and Relationships

Taking many forms, intimacy is a universal need that people receive through relationships. Sexual health requires knowing what intimacy needs are important for the individual, and finding appropriate ways to meet these needs.

Spirituality, Values and Sexual Health

When there is sexual health, there is consistency between one's ethical, spiritual and moral beliefs and one's sexual behaviors. Spirituality may include identification with a formal religion but it doesn't have to.

Keeping the End in Mind

When you start a marathon race, your focus is not on the first mile. Rather it is on completing the entire race and planning how you will survive all 26 miles. In the same way, it is important to have the end of therapy in mind. We not so jokingly start out an early therapy session with a new client by affirming that our goal is to work our self out of a job. We ask them to think about what it would look like to be done with treatment. Often, people often do not have an answer, which is OK at this point of treatment. The question, nevertheless, frames the therapeutic relationship as time limited, goal focused and conscious of the client's goal. Although formal therapy might be complete, the life process has only begun.

As in any treatment program, understanding what the end goals are will help you achieve them. In this case, we are looking to achieve two goals:

1. Reduce your Immediate Short-term Unhealthy Behaviors

Our first goal is to help you understand your "acting-out cycle" by identifying primary high-risk situations, feeling triggers and thinking errors. Through this process, you can reduce the raw number of compulsive behaviors. The topics will explain the concepts and help you apply them to your experience. In addition to eliminating the unhealthy behaviors, the assignments will address related risk factors that may be relevant to your online sexually compulsive patterns.

2. Develop Healthy Sexual Behaviors.

Eliminating unhealthy behaviors creates a void. To maintain long-term health, you'll need to fill this void by practicing healthy sexual behaviors. The assignments in this workbook will help you understand yourself better, provide extensive information that encourages healthy sexual choices, facilitate your journey to define appropriate sexual behaviors, and help you review any possible barriers that get in the way of living a life you love.

Structure of the Assignments

Going back to the image of the marathon race, the goal is to complete the race. The actual path to the goal is the route taking you through places you've probably never seen. To achieve the workbook goals, the structure of the process will take you through the following three stages:

Stage 1 - Problem Identification

During this stage, you will have opportunities to examine your online sexual behaviors and assess the level of compulsiveness. You will complete a number of assignments examining your sexual history and your acting-out cycle. Based on your findings, you will identify the major topics to address in your journey toward improved sexual health.

Stage 2 - Primary Treatment

Once you identify the acting-out cycle in Stage 1, the second stage of treatment helps you begin the work on the major topics within this cycle. You'll do this by completing assignments and resources for the most frequently identified topics. Not every topic you identified may be included, so you may need to address them with your support network. Moreover, in reviewing the topics in this workbook, you may identify additional topics that contribute to your acting-out cycle, but were previously unrecognized.

Stage 3 - Groundwork for Completing Treatment

Stage 3 attempts to stabilize the growth and movement toward sexual health you began in Stage Two. Here you will continue to reach out to others, obtain support and encouragement, and increase accountability. You will also be encouraged to think about living a life you love and the impact of sexual health in helping you create personal fulfillment. This involves clarifying your Internet behavior plan.

The tone of this workbook is conversational, as if we were sitting together during a counseling session, discussing the topics. Within each topic are clear-cut tasks designed to help increase your ability to cope with cybersex issues. Space is provided to answer the questions as you move through the workbook. As you go through the assignments, you may find that some do not apply to you. Please adapt the process to your particular needs. In other words, feel free to complete only those assignments that are necessary for you. However, we encourage you to review each assignment and not simply dismiss the topic. You can learn more when you ask yourself, "How does this topic apply to me?" than when you simply ask, "Does this topic apply to me?" If the topic fits, you will need to follow-up as necessary. The material in each topic is merely an introduction to the issue; each topic could be a workbook in its own right.

As a note of caution, you may experience various levels of personal distress while working on the assignments, such as embarrassment, shame or guilt. This is typical in any personal growth process. We recommend that you have a support system – such as a therapist, sponsor or self-help group – to help smooth the progress of your work.

A Program of Integrity

It is easy to imagine how many people desire their clinician to be in charge. We cannot tell you how many times we've heard, "Tell me what to do," "Is this OK?" or "What should be my bottom-line behavior?" As clinicians, we provide feedback and suggestions, but impose very few behavioral restrictions. When we do, the restrictions are usually around legal, ethical or health consequences. We might say, "Engaging in anonymous sex with individuals whom you have met online probably isn't consistent with what you say you want," or, "Using the work computer to look at porn may get you fired."

This workbook will not tell you what to do, or have you follow a predetermined pattern of required rules. To fall into the trap of telling you right from wrong sets up the therapist as the external control. In motivational psychology, a long-term consequence of external control is a decrease in compliance with the external limits. Slowly, resentment builds as the individual "fights" with those external limits. Eventually a total break may occur where the client's resistance causes a rupture in the therapeutic relationship.

Rather, our treatment approach emphasizes integrity. The approach implies an internal source of control. Research in motivational psychology has repeatedly demonstrated that individuals will create profound changes and new possibilities when internally motivated; they will, for example, run marathons because they want to make a difference in the world. Think for a moment about someone who inspires you; this person's source of motivation is probably internally focused.

Our treatment approach helps you create integrity in your life. The goal is to help identify behaviors, attitudes and goals that lead to wholeness, completeness and unity. This approach, however, requires more work than simply following a list of rules. It also requires some trial and error that results in a reassessment of how you want to live your life. Following this approach, you can create an internal moral code of sexual health. You'll be happier, more effective and ultimately "whole." In the end, the treatment approach requires from you a transformation rather than a compliance with a set of rules. In this transformation, unlimited possibilities are achievable, including living a life you love.

How (NOT) to use this book

If you choose, you could finish this workbook in a few hours (or even less) by simply writing down quick responses to the questions. That approach, however, is not productive. This book is designed for reflection. Pay attention to the concepts of discernment and integrity. Be honest and thorough. Don't edit your responses. Simply write. If issues arise as you answer the questions, you can address them in due time. Space is available throughout the workbook, although in some cases you may need additional paper.

Discernment

Discernment is the exercise of discovering, and revealing the truth within you. Discernment is a process. Although the first response to a question might "seem" like the "correct" response, discovering your personal truth occasionally requires additional time. Often we edit or limit our thoughts, beliefs and desires. Discovering your deeper self requires you to challenge the thoughts, beliefs and values you assume to be true. Self-identity is about integrating results from many trials and errors, experimentation, successes and failures.

Discernment is also about responsibility. It requires you to step-up and say, "This is important. This is what I believe." Too often, people avoid this responsibility for any number of fears including fear of judgment, or disapproval. Paradoxically, when you step-up and take responsibility for your journey, freedom is possible resulting in a feeling of empowerment to say, "Yes, this is me!"

Additional Resources

David Delmonico and Elizabeth Griffin have co authored a book with Dr. Patrick Carnes entitled, *In the Shadows of the Net, Breaking Free of Compulsive Online Sexual Behavior.* This book can be an additional resource for you as you continue on your journey of finding sexual health in an electronic world. David and Elizabeth also have a website with a number of resources that may be helpful to you as well, www. Internetbehavior.com

Much of the material in this workbook was also posted in draft form on Weston Edwards' blog located at: http://sexualhealthinstitute.blogspot.com. His first workbook, *Living a Life I Love*, focuses on general sexual compulsivity. Since publication, the purpose of the blog became a place to add material, provide reactions and comments and to serve as a starting point for conversation. Too many people are isolated and have no place to engage in these conversations. Please feel free to review the blog for new material. If you have a specific question, please visit the blog. We may use it as a question to frame a post.

There are additional online resources that may be of help. We recommend the Society for Advancement of Sexual Health, www.sash.net, which is just one resource where you can find a mental health professional to help facilitate your growth process. Another resource with a number of sexuality educators/resources is www.AASECT.ORG. Always bear in mind that a good therapist respects your personal integrity, appropriately challenges your thoughts and behaviors, and guides you through the therapeutic process.

The Importance and Limits of Confidentiality and Risk of Disclosure

Trust is a major component of counseling. Trust builds a sense of safety that leads to tremendous therapeutic change. Knowing that any information you share will not be told to others strengthens trust. In any therapeutic relationship, confidentiality limits what a professional can disclose to others. You are the one holding this privilege. Depending on where you live, however, there are limits to this privilege. Often the limits facilitate safety in the broad sense of the term, such as requiring the professional to report any suspected abuse of a child or vulnerable adult; significant and real potential harm to yourself (e.g., if you make statements such as "I'm going to kill myself"); significant and real potential harm to another person (e.g., if you makes statements such as "I'm going to kill that person"); or when a court order requires the release of information.

As you complete the assignments, it is important to be open and honest about your past and present behaviors. While it is important for disclosure to occur, it is important for disclosure to occur in a prudent manner. Be careful when making disclosures of sexual behavior. Seriously consider whether your disclosure could trigger a mandatory report as required by the state and local laws where you live. There may be a risk of legal consequences if some of your sexual behaviors include illegal behaviors. One way to ensure privacy and confidentiality is to be specific about behaviors, but not provide any identifiable information. For example, you might want to say "Sexual partner #1" instead of giving the person's full name. It is worth repeating that the goal is to be as honest to yourself and your therapist/support network as possible, while ensuring your own safety.

Finally, consider the security of the workbook. You are encouraged to write in the workbook as you progress through the assignments. Pay attention to who has access to the workbook and where you leave it. It might be helpful to have a conversation with your partner about respecting your privacy.

Disclosure to Partners

We recommend any disclosure to partners occur at the end of the process of working through the workbook. Please share with your partner the conversation that occurs on page 180. Disclosure is a mutual healing process that requires information from your partner as well. There are ideas and assignments for your partner to consider.

Stage 1: The Problem Identification Stage

During this stage, you will have opportunities to examine your online sexual behaviors and assess the level of compulsiveness. However, first you will have a chance to establish a short-term prevention plan in order to begin the process of managing your cybersex behavior. There are eighteen primary topics in this section that will assist you in determining how out of control you are with your cybersex behaviors, assist you with understanding your acting out cycle as well as the various components of your thinking errors, feeling triggers and high-risk situations associated with your acting-out behavior. Based on your findings, you'll be able to identify the major issues for you to address in Stage Two in your journey toward improved sexual health. This may seem scary, but in the end it will help you in your healing.

Immediate Short-Term Prevention Plan

Often what brings a person to therapy is the fact that there are immediate behaviors interfering in that person's life. These behaviors need to be stopped right away before any additional consequences (legal, emotional, relational) occur. Because you purchased this book, there must be some online sexual behaviors that you are concerned about (or someone you care about is concerned about you.). The concerning behavior is what we refer to as the Red Zone behavior – those behaviors that should stop immediately to prevent further self-destruction. Here are a couple questions to help you figure out your Internet Red Zone sexual behaviors:

- What online sexual behaviors prompted you to open this book and begin to read?
- Which of your online sexual behaviors are considered illegal?
- Which online sexual behaviors would you never want anyone else to know about?
- Examples of answers from those who struggle with online sexual behavior include:
  - Spending too much money for online sex.
  - Worrying I might get arrested for looking at child pornography.
  - Unable to stop looking at fetish websites.

- Spending too much time trying to arrange offline sex through the Internet.
- Unable to stop my online sex behavior, in spite of all the consequences.
- Worrying I might act on my Internet fantasies in real life.

This is just a start to get you thinking about your Red Zone behaviors. The reality is that Red Zone behaviors almost always have negative consequences associated with them. We will explore more about your Red Zone online behaviors in the assignment section. Next, we'll discuss some strategies to help manage the Red Zone in the short-term.

The first and most effective management strategy is Internet abstinence. That is, don't ever log on to the Internet again as long as you live. However, this is probably not realistic. Sometimes individuals find taking a short break – a week, a month, or a couple months – away from using the Internet is a helpful alternative place to start. Sometimes people take a break from the Internet at home, while still using it at work, etc. Abstinence can be a great strategy for getting a handle on how out of control your online sexual behavior really is. If your online sex is out of control, it will become clearer during the abstinence period. So, while you may not stop using the Internet everywhere and forever, consider a period of abstinence to get yourself focused. Once the abstinence period is over (or if you decided you couldn't do one), you will need to employ some strategies to manage your online sexual behavior. Here are some simple, yet effective suggestions for managing your online behavior.

- Ensure your computer is only used in high traffic areas.
- Limiting the days/times of use (e.g., not to be used after 11:00pm).
- Limit the amount of time spent on the computer each day (e.g., no more than 1 hour).
- Using the computer only when others are nearby (e.g., not when home alone).
- Specifying locations where the Internet can / cannot be used (e.g., not at hotels).
- Making sure the monitor is visible to others (e.g., co-workers, boss, partner)
- Place screen savers/backgrounds of important people (e.g., family, partner).
- Using only a computer, and not other devices (e.g., iPad).
- Shutting off the data plan on your cell phone.
- Can you think of other strategies that have worked for you?

Your first assignment is to create a list of your Red Zone behaviors. You'll focus on the behaviors you feel you need to stop now. (As an example, in medical triage, you treat the most important issues first. When someone is bleeding, you do not worry about a temperature until you've first stopped the bleeding.) Keep the list handy, since you may discover/remember more as you continue through the workbook. Read over the list slowly and carefully – this is the first step in stopping your behaviors. These Red Zone behaviors do not define who you are, they are simply things you do. Just like any other behavior change, it will not be easy, but at least you are getting a handle on the problem.

Your List of Red Zone Behaviors

- What online sexual behaviors prompted you to open this book and begin to read?

- Are any of your online sexual behaviors considered illegal?

- Which online sexual behaviors would you never want anyone else to know about?

- Examples of answers from those who struggle with online sexual behavior include (explain any that apply):

- Spending (too much) money for online sex.

- Worrying I might get arrested for looking at child pornography.

- Unable to stop looking at fetish websites.

- Spending too much time trying to arrange offline sex through the Internet.

- Unable to stop my online sex behavior, in spite of all the consequences.

- Worrying I might act on my Internet fantasies in real life.

Next, you will develop a list of computer/ Internet management strategies. This is where your honesty will need to play an important role. You need to develop these strategies keeping in mind that at some point you will want to sabotage the list. What strategies will work best for you, even in the face of your own self-sabotage? Even if all the plans don't work 100%, you will be further ahead than when you started. If the plan works…great…if not, regroup and figure out how to improve it. A behavior analysis (see page 71) can help determine the "best new path" if you need one. Don't view this as success or failure - you will be able learn from the process to uncover your unique components to the acting-out cycle (see page 42) and help you strengthen your plans. Which of the following suggestions are you willing to try? Explain your responses.

- Ensure the computer is only used in high traffic areas.

- Limiting the days/times of use (e.g., not to be used after 11:00pm).

- Limit the amount of time spent on the computer each day (e.g., no more than 1 hour).

- Using the computer only when others are nearby (e.g., not when home alone).

- Specifying locations where the Internet can / cannot be used (e.g., not at hotels).

- Making sure monitor is visible to others (e.g., co-workers, boss, partner).

- Placing screen savers / backgrounds of important people (e.g., family, partner, etc.).

- Using only a computer, and not other devices (e.g., iPad).

- Shutting off the data plan on your cell phone.

- Can you think of other strategies that have worked for you?

Do I Have a Problem with Cybersex?

Now we will help you look more closely at your use of sexually explicit material on the Internet. You may be wondering when or even if using the Internet for sex is a real problem.

You might now be asking yourself, "Do I have a problem with my sexual use of the Internet?" "How would I know if there's a problem?" "Am I at risk for sexually problematic behavior on the Internet?" or "Just what is 'problematic' sexual behavior on the Internet?"

Internet Sex Screening Test

One way to help determine if a behavior is problematic is to take a self-administered screening test. The Internet Sex Screening Test has been taken by thousands of individuals and can be used to help gauge how problematic your online sexual behavior may be. Take the test, and then we'll talk more about it later in this section (see next page).

Directions: Read each statement carefully. If the statement is mostly TRUE, place a check mark on the blank next to the item number. If the statement is mostly FALSE, skip the item and place nothing next to the item number.

___1.I have some sexual sites bookmarked.

___2.I spend more than 5 hours per week using my computer for sexual pursuits.

___3.I have joined sexual sites to gain access to online sexual material.

___4.I have purchased sexual products online.

___5.I have searched for sexual material through an Internet search tool.

___6.I have spent more money for online sexual material than I planned.

___7. Internet sex has sometimes interfered with my certain aspects of my life.

___8.I have participated in sexually related chats.

___9. I have a sexualized username or nickname that I use on the Internet.

___10 I have masturbated while on the Internet.

___11 I have accessed sexual sites from other computers besides my home.

___12 No one knows I use my computer for sexual purposes.

___13 I have tried to hide what is on my computer or monitor so others cannot see it.

___14 I have stayed up after midnight to access sexual material online.

___15 I use the Internet to experiment with different aspects of sexuality (e.g., bondage, homosexuality, anal sex, etc.)

___16 I have my own website which contains some sexual material.

___17 I have made promises to myself to stop using the Internet for sexual purposes.

___18 I sometimes use cybersex as a reward for accomplishing something. (e.g., finishing a project, stressful day, etc.)

___19 When I am unable to access sexual information online, I feel anxious, angry, or disappointed.

___20 I have increased the risks I take online (give out name and phone number, meet people offline, etc.)

___21 I have punished myself when I use the Internet for sexual purposes (e.g., time-out from computer, cancel Internet subscription, etc.)

___22 I have met face to face with someone I met online for romantic purposes.

___23 I use sexual humor and innuendo with others while online.

___24 I have run across illegal sexual material while on the Internet.

___25 I believe I am an Internet sex addict.

___26 I repeatedly attempt to stop certain sexual behaviors and fail.

___27 I continue my sexual behavior despite it having caused me problems.

___28 Before my sexual behavior, I want it, but afterwards I regret it.

___29 I have lied often to conceal my sexual behavior.

___30 I believe I am a sex addict.

___31 I worry about people finding out about my sexual behavior.

___32 I have made an effort to quit a certain type of sexual activity and have failed.

___33 I hide some of my sexual behavior from others.

___34 When I have sex, I feel depressed afterwards.

What is Problematic Behavior?

What does the word "problematic" even mean? When a particular behavior or a set of behaviors interferes with other aspects of your life, psychologists, psychiatrists, and counselors call them problematic, meaning these behaviors are causing problems and jeopardizing important areas in your life. Let's say, for example, you've been using the Internet for sex more than ever lately. You've gone online with the intention of staying there for thirty minutes only to suddenly realize that two or three hours have slipped by. On more than one occasion, this "slipup" had some consequence - once you missed an important business appointment and another time you were late picking up your daughter from soccer. Perhaps you learned of some consequence only later. It's not unusual for people to be unaware of the consequence their actions are having in their own and other people's lives.

When isolated instances like this occur, they probably are not an indication of a problem. However, if they continue or increase, it may be a signal to pay more attention to what is happening. As these behaviors expand and we become aware of them, we may try to avoid or minimize consequences by attempting control the problematic behavior. Unfortunately, during this time it also becomes more difficult to see what is happening and to control our behaviors.

Indicators of Problematic Behavior

The following criteria are indicators of problematic behavior: compulsivity, continuation despite adverse consequences, and obsession. Here are explanations of each:

Compulsivity

This means the loss of the ability to choose whether to stop a behavior. In our daily lives, we establish habit-forming routines. We often get up at the same time every day, brush our teeth in the same way, keep a work area arranged in a particular order, put the same arm into a shirt first when getting dressed, and shop at the same grocery store week after week. We repeat many behaviors, often to the point where they become habits. Habits serve a useful function in that they free us from having to actually think about what we're doing all the time. Imagine how difficult it would be if every single time you began to put on your shirt or brush your teeth, you had to think about how to do these tasks.

Compulsive behavior, however, is altogether different from routine habits. It is out-of-control behavior marked by deeply entangled rituals and obsessions, along with overwhelming feelings of frustration, self-blame, powerlessness, and hopelessness.

Continuation Despite Adverse Consequences

It is common to continue compulsive behavior despite adverse consequences, such as loss of health, job, relationships, marriage, or freedom. All behaviors have consequences.

Most of the time, we are able to look at our behavior and make the appropriate changes to reduce negative consequences. Unfortunately, when compulsive behavior is involved, this isn't the case. Attempts to control the behavior – and the potentially dire consequences – are not working. You want to stop but you feel as though you can't.

Other people might see the direct and indirect negative consequences of your behavior, even though you yourself might not.

Obsession

Obsession means being so preoccupied, you focus exclusively on a particular behavior (in this case, sex) to the exclusion of other parts of your life and without care for the consequences of that behavior. You are obsessed with something when you just can't stop thinking about it. It occupies much of your mental energy most of the time.

You may be living your entire life in one of the three states of mind: planning to sexually act out on the Internet, being online sexually acting out, or coming down, i.e., recovering from sexually acting out online. In one way or another, sexually acting out online is always on your mind.

Do you see how these concepts were represented in the Internet Sex Screening Test? Go back and look at the items, and you will see how many of the questions reflect one of these areas: control, consequence, and obsession. Now that you have a better understanding of what constitutes "problematic," score your Internet Sex Screening Test using the information provided below.

Internet Sex Screening Test Scoring Directions

1. Add up the number of check marks placed in items 1 through 25. Use the following scale to interpret the final number.

1 to 8 = You may or may not have a problem with your sexual behavior on the Internet. You are in a low risk group, but if the Internet is causing problems in your life, seek a professional who can conduct further assessment.

9 to 18 = You are "at-risk" for the your sexual behavior to interfere with significant areas of your life. If you are concerned about your sexual behavior online, and you have noticed consequences as a result of your online behavior, it is suggested that you seek a professional who can further assess and help you with your concerns.

19 + = You are at highest risk for your behavior to interfere and jeopardize important areas of your life (social, occupational, educational, etc.). It is suggested that you discuss your online sexual behaviors with a professional who can further assess and assist you.

2. Items 26 through 34 are an abbreviated version of the Sexual Addiction Screening Test (SAST). These items should be reviewed for general sexual addiction behavior, not specifically for cybersex. Although there is no cutoff scores calculated for these items, a high score on items 1 through 25 paired with a high number of items in 26 through 34 should be seen as an even greater risk for sexual acting out behavior on the Internet.

** Please note: Items 26 through 34 should not be calculated in the total score for part 1.

3. No item alone should be an indicator of problematic behavior. You are looking for a constellation of behaviors, including other data that may indicate a struggle with Internet sexuality. For example, it would not be unusual to have sexual sites

bookmarked, or to have searched for something sexual online, but paired with other behaviors, it may be problematic.

Assignment

Now that you have a better understanding of what constitutes problematic online behavior, and you have your score from the Internet Sex Screening Test, your assignment is to write a paragraph or two about why you DO / DON'T have a problem with your online sexual behavior. Write the paragraph to convince yourself of your position. After all, this is about you and no one else. That said, what do you think others would say about your argument?

Talking About Sex

To start addressing questions of online sexual compulsivity, it is important to reflect on your comfort and ability to talk about sex in general. The goal of this exercise is to 1) assess your ability to talk about sex and sexuality with others, and 2) identify people with whom you can talk about sex. We are confident that your comfort level will increase as you progress through your work.

Answer the following questions:

1. I avoid talking about sex.   YES / NO

2. I talk about my sexuality with my friend(s).   YES / NO

3. I find many sexual matters too upsetting to talk about   YES / NO

4. I talk about my sexuality with my sexual partner(s).   YES / NO

5. I talk about my sexual feelings.   YES / NO

6. I usually feel comfortable discussing my sexual values.   YES / NO

7. I usually feel comfortable discussing topics of a sexual nature. YES / NO

8. I usually feel comfortable discussing my sexuality.   YES / NO

9. Talking about sex is usually a positive experience.   YES / NO

10. It bothers me to talk about sex.   YES / NO

11. I usually feel comfortable discussing my sexual behavior.   YES / NO

12. I feel there will be negative consequences if I talk about
    sex.   YES / NO

Score 1 point for each "NO" on questions # 2, 4–7, 9, 11. Score 1 point for each "YES" on questions # 1, 3, 8, 10, 12

Assignment

• Reflect on the above questions: explain your responses.

• Reflect on your thoughts and feelings as you start this process. Many clients express fear, shame, guilt and hopelessness as they look at all the topics in the workbook. How present are these thoughts and feelings?

• Other clients express feelings of hope and excitement, often because they see a pathway where none had existed previously. How present are these thoughts and feelings?

• Having people in your life to support you in the process of improving your sexual health is important. Developing your support network is a way to increase external accountability. Name four people you could start talking to about sexuality and about your online sexual behaviors. This list could include your spiritual advisor, your sponsor, your therapist, your friends, your colleagues, your partner/spouse or others.

- Write one paragraph summarizing what you would like to share at this time with each person regarding your treatment process for cybersex compulsivity. Four simple strategies for starting the process of developing a support network include:

  - Start small. Say, "I'm now in therapy. I need someone to support me, but I'm not ready to go into full detail right now."

  - Examine who in your life is already supportive. Expand what you might say to the person that increases your self-disclosure. You might say, "I'm working with a therapist in the area of human sexuality."

  - Identify a "big name" celebrity that has "come out" regarding his or her sexual compulsivity or online sexual behavior. This can help you introduce the topic.

  - If you can't share the topic at this time, share some of the negative thoughts or feelings that set you up to act-out. You could share, "I'm really stuck on how negative my thoughts are" or, "I struggle with a lot of shame." Below is space to complete a paragraph statement for you to share with the four people listed below in your initial support network.

1.

2.

3.

4.

Offline and Online Sex History

A natural progression from the exercise of talking about sex is the exercise of talking about your sexual history, both offline and online. As you progress through the process of addressing online sexual compulsivity, it is important to describe accurately and completely your past sexual behavior. This document is a "living document," which means it might be helpful to return periodically to the assignment and add material as you remember pieces of your history.

At first, you may not want to put everything on paper because of what others might think. You cannot treat something that's undisclosed. However, when you are open and honest, you will, in the end, have a better sense of your needs in your treatment process.

When you complete the history, please share the responses with another person, sponsor, therapist or group. However, at this time, we do not recommend disclosing this information to your primary partner (that disclosure will happen near the end of stage 2, see page 180). We do recommend that the person(s) with whom you disclose the information be trustworthy and nonjudgmental. (For your safety, please review the material on limits to confidentiality in the introduction, see page 11.)

Assignment

Complete as thoroughly as possible. Use additional paper as necessary. Update as your remember pieces of your history. For example, when used in a group format, hearing the histories of others can trigger additional memories.

Dating and Relationship Behavior

1. At what age did you begin to date or go out with girls/boys your own age?
2. Describe your level of self-confidence regarding dating.
3. How comfortable did you feel?
4. How attractive did you think you were to others?
5. If you have a same sex attraction, when did you come out to yourself? When did you come out to others?
6. Describe your dating behavior?
7. How do you meet dating partners?
8. How did your self-esteem improve or decrease as you dated more frequently?
9. Review the pattern of your relationships:
   a. Describe the number of your relationships, and the type and length of each relationship.
   b. Describe the dating/courtship that occurred in the relationship.
   c. Describe how you met these partners and how you broke up, and discuss any primary concerns you have.
   d. How quickly did sexual contact occur in the relationship?

Sexual Behavior

1. How old were you when you first had sexual intercourse?
2. How old was your partner?
3. How did you feel about the experience?
4. How many sexual partners have you had?
   a. Fill out a table that includes each partner, to the best of your ability.

Your Age	Partner's Age	Type of Sexual Contact	Where	Length of Relationship Plus Other details
16	15	Vaginal sex, oral sex	Both Parents House. Friends House.	Dated for 12 months
22	21	Vaginal sex	Hotel	1 encounter

   a. Describe what behaviors occurred. Be explicit and thorough (e.g. oral sex, vaginal sex, anal sex, mutual masturbation, kissing, touching, etc.).
   b. Describe the location (home, bedroom, public space, bathhouse, bar, etc.).
   c. What was the length of the relationship (one-night stand, occasional or casual sexual encounters that lasted a few months, longtime partnership, six-year marriage, etc.)?
   d. What percentage of all your sexual partners were one-night stands?

e. Describe the circumstances in which you met your sexual partners.
f. How many sexual partners of the same sex as yourself have you had?
   i. How did you feel about it then?
   ii. How do you feel about it now?
g. Describe the frequency and circumstances of sexual encounters that occurred while using drugs and/or alcohol?
h. If your number of sexual partners is too large to count, complete the assignment by examining periods of your life and estimating the number of contacts. Pick periods that make sense to you. For example:
   i. Up to age 13 (pre-adolescence), number of partners_____
   ii. Age 14–18, number of partners_____
   iii. Age 19–24, number of partners_____
   iv. First Job, number of partners_____
   v. At the time of your first significant relationship, number of partners_____
   vi. After divorce and/or end of first relationship, number of partners_____
   vii. At the time you lived at a particular address or a particular city, number of partners_____
   viii. Describe any patterns you've noticed as you complete this section.

5. Describe the frequency and circumstances of sexual contact with someone else other than your primary partner while you were married or in a committed relationship.
6. Describe any circumstances where you have intentionally avoided sexual contact with a partner or significant other. Include any underlying thoughts and feelings.

Masturbation

1. At what age did you first masturbate?
2. How did you learn about masturbation?
3. What messages did you hear about masturbation while growing up?
4. What were your beliefs and feelings about masturbation while growing up?
5. What are your beliefs and feelings about masturbating today?
6. How often do you masturbate (focus on the last 30 days)?
7. When was the last time you masturbated?
8. What thoughts and feelings did you have when you last masturbated?

9. Describe the frequency and circumstances when you masturbated somewhere other than your home?
10. When you masturbate, what objects have you used to enhance your level of sexual arousal (e.g. items of clothing, vibrators, magazines, sexual toys, items to inflict pain)? Describe the items and circumstances of their use for sexual stimulation.

Fantasy

1. Describe your three most arousing sexual fantasies.
2. How do you feel about these fantasies?
3. What messages and beliefs did you hear about having sexual fantasies?
4. What beliefs do you have about sexual fantasies today?
5. Have you ever masturbated to sexual fantasies of rape? If so, describe the fantasy, including your relationship to the victim/abuser, the frequency of the fantasy and the length of time since your last rape fantasy.

Health Concerns

1. Describe the frequency of physical problems you have experienced that affect your ability to be sexual (such as difficulties achieving or maintaining erections, difficulties having orgasms, a lack of interest in sex, difficulties in delaying ejaculation, painful penetration), and then describe the circumstances in which you experienced these difficulties.
2. Describe the frequency with which you've contracted sexually transmitted infections and the circumstances under which you were infected. How was the infection transmitted?
3. Describe any circumstances leading to pregnancy, bearing a child or being the partner of someone who became pregnant or bore a child.
4. Describe any circumstances leading to having an abortion or being the partner of someone who had an abortion.

Abuse

1. Describe the frequency of being sexually touched or being forced to engage in sexual behavior as a child. Describe the circumstances under which these instances occurred.

2. Describe the frequency of being sexually touched or being forced to engage in sexual behavior as an adult. Describe the circumstances under which these instances occurred.
3. Describe the frequency of being the target of sexual harassment, and circumstances under which these instances occurred.
4. Describe the frequency of sexual contact between you and members of your family, and describe the circumstances under which these instances occurred.
5. Describe any circumstances when you abused or sexually harassed someone else.

Children

1. Describe any sexual contact you have had with children while you were an adult.
2. Describe the content of sexually explicit pictures of children you have seen or possessed.
3. Describe the frequency of viewing explicit child sexual material and the circumstances under which you did so.
4. Have you masturbated to fantasies of sex with children? If so, describe the details.

Legal

1. Describe any legal consequences of your sexual behavior.
2. Describe the frequency of legal consequences.

Other Patterns of Sexual Behavior

1. Describe the frequency of paying money for sex or trading drugs for sex, and the circumstances under which you've done so.
2. Describe the frequency of engaging in prostitution and the circumstances under which you've done so.
3. Describe the frequency of having sexual touch with an animal, and the circumstances under which you've done so.
4. Describe the frequency of public sex, exposing your genitals to others without their consent and the circumstances under which you've done so.
5. Describe the frequency of spying on someone for sexual gratification and the circumstances under which you've done so.

6. Describe the types of sexual magazines and movies you view for sexual stimulation.
7. Describe your frequency of using threats of violence, physical force or any weapon to make someone perform a sexual act. Describe the circumstances under which you've done so.
8. Describe the frequency of participating in consensual use of restraints or consensual bondage acts, and describe the circumstances under which you've done so.
9. Describe the frequency of participating in group sex and the circumstances under which you've done so.
10. Describe the frequency of participating in alternative ("kinky") behaviors and the circumstances under which you've done so.

Internet Related Sexual Behaviors

1. At what age did you first start using the Internet for sexual purposes? Describe the behavior and content of your first sexual online sexual experiences.
2. Describe how your frequency of using the Internet for sex changed over the years. Describe any unusual patterns.
3. Describe when you have become sexually aroused while engaging in Internet sexual behaviors. What type of activity were you involved in at the time?
4. Describe what you enjoy doing most sexually online, (e.g., looking at pornography, visiting chat rooms, exposing yourself)? How has this preference changed over time?
5. Describe the frequencies and areas of sexual activity that you enjoy exploring online, (e.g., certain ethnicities, feet, animals, diapers…).
6. Have you ever done anything sexually online that could be considered illegal? Describe in a general way.
7. Describe the frequency and circumstances where you have used virtual worlds such as Second Life to engage in virtual sex.
8. Describe the frequency and circumstances when you have used the Internet to arrange for an escort service or prostitute?
9. Describe the frequency of using the Internet to meet sexual partners and the circumstances under which you used the Internet to make these connect
10. Describe the frequency and circumstances on how your offline sexuality has been impacted by your online sexual behaviors?

11. Describe the frequency and circumstances when you posted online erotic or sexual pictures/videos of yourself or others (including via webcam or texting).
12. Describe the frequency and circumstances when you masturbate with online sexual materials or activities. What type of content do you typically masturbate to?
13. Describe any "ritual" you may engage in regards to your Internet sex use (e.g., planning and preparing the same way each time, cleaning/deleting files after each Internet sex session, etc.)?
14. Describe the frequency and circumstances when you have engaged in high-risk behaviors while online (e.g., downloading pornography at work, engaged in illegal online behaviors, etc.) What is the typical content of such materials?
15. Describe the frequency and circumstances when you engaged in cybersex behavior at work or at the houses of friends or relatives.
16. Describe the frequency and circumstances when you had any physical problems as a result of your Internet sexual behavior (e.g., contracted an STD from a chat partner, been injured by a sex partner met online, etc.).
17. Describe the frequency and circumstances when you used a sex toy that connects to your computer while online?
18. What other sexual activities have you engaged while online that would be important to disclose?

General

1. Describe any sexual behaviors or practices that are not addressed in the above questions.
2. Which three questions from the section above were the most difficult to answer?
    a. Why did you select these three questions?
    b. What made them so difficult to answer?
3. What are three things you learned about yourself by completing this assignment?
4. Which three areas would you highlight at this time as the primary areas of concern?

Internet Sexual Behavior Timeline

The goal of this exercise is to translate the material from your sex history into a visual format. In creating your Internet Sexual Behavior Timeline, you will be concentrating on your Internet sexual behavior, making it possible for you to understand how your sexual behaviors on the Internet have occurred across time in relation with other issues. By charting these events, you can discover patterns in your online sexual behavior. Although it is possible to see a relationship between behaviors and other issues, it is not possible to determine cause and effect. Using the Internet to act-out sexually might be an attempt to cope with anxiety or depression, or conversely it may actually be the cause of your anxiety or depression. By completing the Sexual Behavior Timeline, you may get a sense of the various relationships that exist between your emotions and your online

Complete the following exercise as thoroughly as possible. Use the information from the previous sexual history exercise and plot the events along the horizontal timeline (see sample timeline below), attempting to reflect on your age at the time of the event. In addition to the behaviors identified in your sexual history, plot the following life events on the time line. (See the next page for additional instructions.)

- Age when you hit puberty.

- The first time you:

  - Masturbated.
  - Masturbated at a computer.
  - Remember being attracted to another person.
  - Had an orgasm.
  - Had sex with anyone.
  - Used the Internet for sexual purposes.
  - Kept your online sexual behavior hidden.
  - Felt shame regarding your online sexual behavior.

- Age at relationship changes (new relationship, divorce, breakup, entering into marriage/partnership, etc.)

- Age at life changes (home move, new job, substance-abuse treatment, sobriety, first child, illness, death of a loved one, etc.).

- Any critical incidents in your life. A critical incident is any event, large or small, that has meaning in your life. (Examples: when you first self-identified as gay, the time you were sexually assaulted.).

- Any and all online sexual activity, especially times when your online sexual behavior increased or decreased in frequency, intensity, and/or behaviors

- With color pens or pencils, track relevant behaviors. This might include tracking spending behaviors, drug or alcohol behaviors, gambling, etc. (See Acting-out and Other Compulsive Behaviors, page 65). Also, track additional life events such as depression or mood changes, stress, relationship satisfaction, job satisfaction or other important events in your life, especially as they relate to your online sexual behavior. Below is a simplified example to illustrate how to complete a timeline. Please feel free to adapt as necessary.

It might be helpful to tape a few pieces of paper together or use poster board to increase your space. Across the left-hand edge of the page, draw a vertical line. The vertical line should be numbered +5 to 0. At the center of the vertical line, draw a horizontal line that travels the length of the page. The horizontal line reflects your age across time. If you notice, the space on the timeline is not "equal." Some parts of your life are less relevant, so you can save space. Other times of your life may be more expansive.

You might need to devise a code to fit everything into the timeline. Some clients have used multiple colors to chart a number of items. For some people this might be mood or chemical use or anxiety, or whatever. If, for example, at the time of a marriage you were very happy, your mood might be charted at a +5. One client charted both the amount of chemical use and mood. Afterward he was able to see the inverse relationship between mood and chemical use. The more he used, the lower his mood. Admittedly, the timeline does not necessarily show causality. His lower mood may have contributed to his increased chemical use as an attempt to self-medicate to cope with the online sexual behavior

Below the line are spaces to describe relevant events in your life. The key for the bottom part of the timeline is to examine life events and topics to see how they fit into the picture. Each timeline will be different. You are literally creating a graph of your life. What is relevant to each person varies as much as each individual. In this example, we had three items; your timeline might have more. Additional topics to graph include financial, relational, geographic and/or familial changes.

Sample Time Line

+5	
+4	Graph the intensity of important feelings such as grief, depression, anger, loneliness, etc. +5 very intense, 0 Not present.
+3	
+2	
+1	
0	

Write out the major components of your sex history along this line

Include major life events in your life. It is helpful to write small.

Age	10	12	13	18	19
Relevant Life History Info	Parents divorced	Went to JH	Felt isolated from classmates	College	Failed out of college
Online Sexual Behavior History	Saw porn for the first time on the Internet	Begin getting up in the middle of the night to look at online porn	Gave up soccer because wanted to have more time to look at Internet porn	Porn use increased both in time and graphic, bizarre nature	Looking at porn and masturbating online for more than 8 hours a day
Chemical History Info		Begin sneaking beer from house	Started to drink when looking at porn	Binge drinking	Begin using pot. Hooked up with someone who had meth.

Types of Online Sexual Users - Who Are You?

At this point you should begin understanding your online sexual behavior. Understanding the various types of online line sexual users should assist you in determining how problematic your online sexual behavior is in your life. It is important to know that not everyone who uses the Internet for sexual activities does so for the same reason or to the same extent, and that not all cybersex has negative consequences. We have divided those who are engaging in sexual behavior on the Internet into five groups, illustrated by the diagram below.

Cybersex User Categories

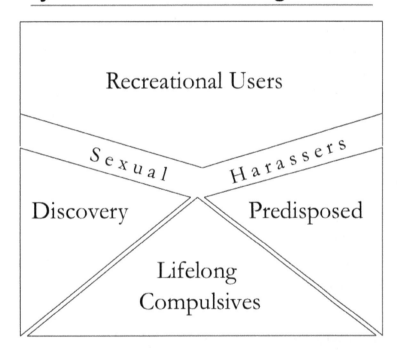

Recreational Cybersex Users

Recreational cybersex users are divided into two categories: appropriate recreational users and inappropriate recreational users. The former seem to be able to explore sex on the Internet without any sign of their behavior becoming problematic. Their behavior is out in the open, not covert. Time spent in cybersex behaviors is minimal, usually totaling no more than a couple of hours a week. They do not feel embarrassed or shameful about these activities, and often they take part in them with their spouse or partner. They may, in fact, use cybersex as a way to enhance their sexual experience with one another and thus to strengthen their relationship.

Sexual Harassers

There is an "in-between" of individuals who don't have a cybersex problem, but still engage in behaviors that may be a concern. We classify this group as recreational group users. The latter group of recreational cybersex users includes individuals who do not have a compulsive or addictive problem with sex on the Internet, but who use what they find on the Internet inappropriately. They may, for example, show a sex-related item or site they discovered on the Internet to others such as their work colleagues, family members, or friends who are not interested in such information or who are embarrassed by it. They do so, not as a means of hurting or embarrassing others, but simply because they think such information is funny or because they like the feeling of shocking others. These individuals who use cybersex inappropriately don't try to hide their activities either, whereas people who have a more serious problem with cybersex go to great lengths to cover up their cybersex activities from others in their lives. While these behaviors may be inappropriate, individuals can easily be redirected when confronted with their behavior.

Problematic Cybersex Users

The bottom half of the diagram highlights individuals with problematic behaviors. People who exhibit problematic sexual behavior on the Internet tend to fall into one of the three groups:

Discovery Group

People in this group have no previous problem with online sex and no history of problematic offline sexual behavior. However they often begin using sex on the Internet as a recreational user and become completely carried away with his or her online activities, spending many hours at his or her computer.

Predisposed Group

This group is made up of people who have never acted out sexually (though they have thought about it) until they discovered cybersex. They might have fantasized about exposing themselves or had the urge to see a prostitute or go to a strip club. Until they discovered the world of cybersex, however, they were able to manage their fantasies and urges. Maybe they were afraid of being recognized at a strip club or being arrested in a prostitution sting. Perhaps they simply were healthy enough and possessed adequate coping skills to recognize and resist these impulses.

People in this group may use the Internet for sexual purposes less frequently than people in some of the other groups, but they are certainly at risk for more problematic online sexual behavior. With the Internet, sex is just a mouse-click away, and at some point, they discover sexually explicit activities that they just can't resist. At first, the consequences of their cybersex activities may seem minimal. After all, no one will see them or recognize them online.

People in this group often have clear boundaries for their urges or fantasies until they encounter the cyber world, where they feel okay about pushing beyond them. Once that boundary is stretched or breached, little may be left to control behavior.

Lifelong Sexually Compulsive Group

People in this group have been involved in problematic sexual behavior throughout most of their lives. They might compulsively masturbate, compulsively use pornography, practice voyeurism or exhibitionism, or compulsively frequent strip clubs and prostitutes. For these people, cybersex simply provides a new option for acting out sexually that fits within their already existing patterns of problematic behavior.

Assignment

Complete the following questions:

Review the definitions of types of users. How would you describe your use of the Internet?

Review the questions from the Internet Screen Test on page 19 and your Online and Offline Sex History starting on page 27. How has your response to the type of user you might be changed?

How would your support network describe your computer use?

Share your response with your support network and obtain their feedback.

Tracking Your Behavior: Internet Activity Log

Before you can decide how to change your sexual online behaviors, it is important to know exactly what they are. To do this, we ask you to keep a log of all of your online activity (not just your cybersex activity) for two weeks. Include all of your time online at all locations where you use a computer. Also include any online activity on portable devices, such as your cell phone. For now, don't be concerned about changing your behavior, just recording it.

Get a notebook or a journal. For each time you go online record the following:

Date:
Time:

- What did you do on the Internet (WWW, Internet Chat, Social Networking)?
- Where was the computer you used to access the Internet?
- What type of device did you use (computer, iPad, smart phone)?
- What type of sexual behavior occurred? Record the following, as applicable:
  - Describe the sexually explicit pictures you viewed.
  - Describe any sexual chat (include transcript, if available).
  - Describe any sexualizations and sexual fantasies.
  - Describe any masturbation behavior while online.
  - What were you feeling right before going online for sexual purposes?
  - What were you feeling while online engaging in sexual behavior?
  - What were you feeling after being online for sexual purposes?

After keeping this log for a week spend some time analyzing your weekly log. When you analyze your weekly log, you can gain insight into your fantasies, thoughts, experiences and behaviors to uncover various themes. For each thought, experience, behavior or fantasy, complete a behavioral analysis (see page 71).

- What did you learn through the analysis?

- What computer or portable device do you use the most to engage in sexual behavior?

- What did you find arousing during your online sexual experience?

- Whom did you find attractive?

- What thoughts did you have before, during and afterward?

- If it was a fantasy, what did you think and how did you feel about yourself?

- Was the behavior or fantasy healthy or unhealthy?

- Why? Is there a pattern to your use of the Internet for sexual purposes?

- What themes might be present to help you understand yourself better?

Revealing the Problems: The Acting-Out Cycle

The acting-out cycle is a framework to explain how people "act-out" their compulsive behaviors. The entire workbook connects to this cycle. The key to changing the cycle is to first recognize the feeling triggers, high-risk settings, thinking errors, "active and passive" ways of acting-out and the perceived payoffs and consequences. We will review each concept in greater detail, but this brief review will help you develop an initial understanding.

The Acting Out Cycle

Set ups:
Emotional Triggers
Thinking Errors
High Risk Situations

Payoffs / Costs
Rewards /
Consequences

Act Out
Sexual Behavior
Other Types of
Behaviors

Setups

To bake a cookie, first the baker assembles the ingredients. Likewise, in acting-out, first the person assembles the ingredients, or "setups," for the acting-out cycle. Some setups are easily recognized. Most people who struggle with Internet sexual compulsivity can identify various patterns before they act-out. For the sake of simplicity, we have reduced the setups to three types: Feeling Triggers, Thinking Errors and High-Risk Situations. Each will be reviewed in detail in the next topics.

An example illustrates these setups. Let's say a person feels depressed, so he goes online to look at pornography. The feeling of depression, identified in this example, precedes the "acting-out" incident. In the same example, a "thinking error" might also be present: "I'll only go online for 30 minutes and only go to one porn site. It isn't a big deal." The "high-risk situation" is going online when feeling depressed. As you move through the treatment process, you will start to identify additional setups. In the end, you will be able to identify ten to fifteen setups of each type.

Act-Out

The act-out phase of the cycle is the unhealthy behavior. It is often the same as the sexual behavior (for example, I had sex with this person; I watched some porn). What you will recognize is that acting-out doesn't just happen through sexual behavior. In the field of chemical addiction, there is a term called "cross addiction" (we use the term cross compulsivity, see page 65). We work with clients who stop their chemical use but then their sexual behavior gets out of control. Once both the sexual behavior and chemical use are under control, it is not surprising to see another issue develop, such as overeating, compulsive spending or gambling. The key to overall health is to realize that online sexual behavior is only one expression of the acting-out cycle; it is important to understand all the different ways you may act-out. (The goal of the timeline on page 36 is to help you identify your patterns.) In recognizing the range of behaviors you can then address the underlying dynamic of the cycle. This is the only way to avoid a Band-Aid approach to overall health. As we move through the process, you'll discover passive ways of acting-out that are as important as active ways of acting-out. For example, some people withdraw from conflict because of fear. The person then feels resentful, which results in an explosion of anger (another type of acting-out).

Payoffs/Costs

All behavior is goal focused, including acting-out. Payoffs are the perceived or actual outcome of the behavior. In the previous example, the perceived payoff was a relief from depression. As you can probably recognize, the payoff is usually temporary. In fact, sometimes the perceived payoff leads to the cycle starting all over again. It is important to think strategically regarding payoffs. Some payoffs might not be easily recognized at first. Yes, pleasure from viewing pornography might be one payoff, but another payoff might be avoiding the fear of being hurt in a relationship, so the payoff from choosing pornography is being "safe." Costs are more easily recognized. In behavioral terms, we identify these as "consequences." Examples of consequences include, damage to relationships ("My partner is angry about my behavior,") legal ("I was arrested,") and physical ("I got drunk.").

Relationship Between the Components

In the Acting-out Cycle diagram on page 42, the arrows are double pointed. The cycle is dynamic, meaning it is always shifting, moving and adapting. The cycle provides feedback to the individual, and the individual adapts as necessary to continue the cycle. We will review this relationship throughout the exercises. An acting-out encounter may have a consequence that sets the person up to act-out again. Treatment involves working through this cycle and addressing all aspects. You will constantly return to the acting-out cycle through the book. Please make sure you understand the basics at this time. You will continue to grow in your understanding through the next few topics and Stage 2.

Power of Thought

A lot of emphasis in our treatment approach focuses on helping you understand your thinking patterns and, in particular, your "thinking errors." To do so, we first need to discuss the power of thought. [2]The basic premise is that all aspects of our entire existence are based on thought – that thought shapes how we perceive and examine life events, our feelings, and our interactions with others. This section discusses why we believe thought is so powerful.

At one point in the Broadway musical *Wicked*, the heroine enters Oz, where the citizens wear green-colored glasses. Over time, the citizens had just forgotten they were wearing green glasses, and simply concluded that everything was in fact green. This was why Oz appeared to be an "Emerald City." In a similar way, our thinking patterns color our view of life. These patterns are so pervasive that we simply don't realize they are present. Sometimes the assumptions have a limited impact in our lives; other times, these thinking patterns are so unhealthy they result in painful consequences. In many ways, the cultures we belong to are the lenses we use to look at the world. Our awareness of these lenses has disappeared simply because we see through them versus seeing them. Moving toward sexual health means moving toward understanding the cultural lenses we use to understand the world.

Our cultural views shape both our worldview and our experience of each moment. Within each moment our awareness and knowledge are based on perceptions, and through the almost instantaneous analysis of these perceptions, we arrive at a conclusion (i.e., a "thought") that guides our feelings, choices and behaviors. This is a bit different from conventional wisdom, which often dictates that feelings come first. Yet, consider the following scenarios:

You parked your car on the street. As you return from the store, you find your car is gone. The awareness is that your car is missing. The feelings result from the conclusions based on various thoughts. Depending on the thought, your feelings might be different. Consider the following:

> You have been reading the newspaper about stolen cars in the neighborhood. The thought that percolates to your awareness is, "My car has been stolen," and you probably have feelings of anger or of being violated, or both.

> As an alternative, you notice a "No Parking" sign during high traffic/rush hours. You happen to have parked your car just before that time began, and you returned to find you car gone. Your thought might be, "My car has been towed." Notice, however, your feelings are different based on your thoughts. You might feel anger, embarrassment, frustration or shame because you feel you should have known better.

> Consider a third possibility. You're talking on a cell phone, as you get to where you thought you parked your car, you realize it is gone. You think, "My car is gone" with thoughts of anger, violation, frustration, etc. Then you notice that six spaces up is your car. Because you were distracted, you went to the wrong space. The corresponding feelings might be embarrassment, relief, and/or humor as you realize how you overreacted.

These three examples help explain how thoughts shape your feelings and subsequent behaviors. One author highlights how much of our thought is actually automatic and can occur in the blink of an eye[3]. Sometimes we simply don't realize how many different thoughts we have in a particular moment. Not true, you say? Think about how many complicated tasks, thoughts and attention to stimuli occur while you drive a car. Yet, you never *think* about driving a car. You simply drive. Similarly, in treating Internet sexual compulsivity, therapists help clients realize how ritualized the acting-out process is.

Two strategies to use at this point for increasing the awareness of the power of your thoughts are "mindfulness" and "transference." Both are powerful tools that give us insight into the power of thought.

Mindfulness

Mindfulness is the experience of being aware of your current thoughts, feelings, body state and surroundings by paying attention to your reactions, motivations and actions. To increase your ability to be mindful, I encourage you to become aware of your inner conversation. When someone walks into the room, we may say to the person next to us, "She's attractive." But our inner conversation is what we have with ourselves when no one is around. Someone might walk into the room, and we say to ourselves, "I want to have sex with her." Various meditation techniques can also be helpful in increasing your mindfulness. The process of behavioral analysis described later in the stage is a tool of increasing mindfulness by asking you to reflect on your thoughts, feelings and behaviors when you last acted-out (see the section on Behavioral Analysis on page 71).

Transference

Transference is any reaction we have to another person. Often the experience of transference occurs so quickly, we don't realize either that it occurred or the content of the transference. We are CONSTANTLY assessing and judging our environment based on our past experience. It is the past experience applied to the current situation that typifies transference. Most of the time we focus on negative transference, or the negative reactions we have to someone, but positive transference is also helpful to understand. In any reaction, you can learn what you are feeling and thinking and how it relates to your acting-out cycle. The individuals with whom we have the strongest reaction are perhaps the people who can teach us the most. It is your reaction that tells you the most about yourself. Ask yourself the following questions: "Why am I having this reaction? Who does this remind me of? What memory does this person trigger? Why do I like or dislike this person?" Whatever the response, you can gain insight into your internal thoughts and feelings.

Taken together, mindfulness and transference are two important concepts to help you increase your awareness of your thoughts. Much of what we think occurs so automatically that we see the picture but fail to see the pieces of the puzzle. The acting-out cycle is equivalent to the picture, while the thoughts, feelings and high-risk situations are the individual pieces.

The Psychology of the Internet

The psychology of the Internet involves unique assumptions and circumstances that must be confronted in the process toward recovery. The tendency for the behaviors to occur online is due to patterns of thinking that occur as a result of the environment of being on the Internet.

The perceived (and inaccurate) anonymity aspect of the Internet can decrease people's empathy for others both in real-time and in the virtual world online. People realize that they can simply shut off the computer if they believe they are in over their heads, and this belief can lead them to take risks that they wouldn't otherwise take. The environment of the Internet allows behavior to occur online that would be less likely to occur offline. The thought that the behavior is "just a game" and "no one can find me," or that "no one will get hurt" leads people to engage in riskier behaviors.

One "thinking error" (see below) is the belief that the Internet is anonymous, that "no one will find out." At some level, however, EVERYTHING you do is tracked online. One notion is that because so much is occurring online, no one cares. The reality, however, is that EVERY website you visit is tracked by your Internet service provider. Many of the sex content sites track your clicks, length of time on a page, and your interests through cookies that can be used by many companies. Advertising companies on the sex websites track your usage across different websites.

The speed and ease with which online sexual content can be accessed is amazing. Too often, simply typing an inaccurate web address can lead a person to a high-risk website. Simply saying, "I won't go there" doesn't always work due to the amount of material online.

Because of the absence (or lack of) social cues (such as age, sex or economic status) there is sometimes an assumption that we are all equals online. The MSNBC television series *To Catch a Predator* regarding online sexual chat between adults and children dispelled this notion that we are all equals online.

Thinking Errors

The concept of "Thinking Errors" (sometimes referred to as "psychological defenses," "cognitive distortions," or even "stinkin' thinkin'," depending on the theoretical orientation of the clinician) refers to a pattern of unhealthy thinking. Often, these thinking errors are attempts to minimize pain, justify our behaviors, avoid responsibility, or otherwise help us avoid reality. As you increase your awareness of thinking errors, the variety and number of thinking errors will surprise you. You will be amazed at the presence of these thoughts and how we use them to justify almost all behavior. A great place to start recognizing a thinking error is to look at any thought that comes after the word "because." I was online "because . . . or " I was downloading pictures because. . ." While not universal, the vast majority of times we answer "because," we are using a thinking error.

In the movie "Shrek," the ogre Shrek describes ogres as having layers, like onions. ("Onions have layers. Ogres have layers. Onions have layers. You get it? We both have layers!") Like ogres, our thoughts often have deeper layers. As we delve deeper into recognizing our thinking, it is possible to gain insight into deeper levels of meaning. Sometimes even a "great reason" hides a thinking error, so it's important to think outside the box and look at the layers of thought. Take, for example, why a person stops at a stop sign. In asking the question, "What is one reason a person stops at a stop sign?" a number of reasons are possible. A few reasons might be, "I don't want to get a ticket." "I don't want to get hurt." "It is what I'm taught." While true, each reflects a possible deeper level of concern that needs to be uncovered. "I don't want to get in trouble" might reflect layers of guilt/shame. A possible deeper level of concern using safety as an explanation might also reflect layers of anxiety. For some people, they don't stop at stop signs. Rather, they sort of "roll through them." This can also reflect a pattern of thinking such as "the rules don't apply to me." As a fun exercise, the next time you are driving, ask yourself the reason you are stopping at the next stop sign you come across.

As illustrated in the acting-out cycle (see page 42), and in the Power of Thought discussion above, our thoughts shape our reality. We act based on thoughts. Often we hear comments such as "I didn't know what I was thinking" or "I knew I shouldn't be doing this, so why couldn't I stop myself?" Our response as therapists is to affirm that the acting-out cycle is insidious: people will act on thoughts they may not fully realize are present. The speed of our thoughts is simply too fast for us to fully understand them before we act. Some of these thoughts might be suppressed or repressed. Others may be so automatic we simply don't recognize their power. An important purpose of therapy is to help you reveal the unhealthy thinking patterns in your life.

A summary of thinking errors follows below, but we must state that *in no way is this list exhaustive*. The mind is an amazingly creative source of never-ending thinking errors, and these examples represent just the most frequent types. One of our main goals is to help you become aware of the various thinking patterns in your life.

List of Frequent Thinking Errors

Justification: Making excuses for our behaviors.
"I deserved it."
"It happened to me and no one cared, so why should I care?"
"I was angry, so my behavior is understandable."
"It's what I like, so the other person should like it too."
"My partner isn't available, so it's OK to be online."
"I've been working all day at the computer, I deserve a 5-minute surfing break."

Displacement/Blaming: Telling ourselves someone or something else is responsible for our actions.
"If she had not done what she did, nothing bad would have happened."
"He started it."
"The web page kept popping up on its own; I didn't know how to stop it."
"I was only downloading adult porn, I didn't want the child porn."
"She had a reputation, so she deserved it."
"He didn't tell me to stop, so it was his fault."
"She's started sexually chatting with me, so it was as much her fault as mine."

Minimization: Playing down the nature of the discretion or the harm.
"I only did it this one time."
"It was only a fantasy, I didn't actually touch her."
"The Internet is just a fantasy world, everyone does this."
"Things just got out of hand."

"It wasn't sex."

"I'll only do it one last time."

"I didn't actually connect with someone."

"It was just chatting"

"It's just pictures; no one was hurt."

Denial: Refusal to accept external reality because it is too threatening.

"I didn't know it was against the law."

"I won't get caught."

"No body will know I'm visiting this website."

"I didn't think my partner would care."

Catastrophizing/Exaggerating: Exaggerating the reasons for or the consequences of our actions. Use of the phrases "the worst," "the best," etc.

"If I hadn't done it, something awful would have happened."

"I did what I did because I had the worst family."

"It was worth it because it was the best sexual encounter ever."

"He was the meanest guy."

Using dramatic gestures and vocalizations such as verbal sighs, waving hands.

Over-Generalization: Use of terms such as "everybody," "never," "always," "no one."

"*Everybody* is online doing sexual stuff."

"I am *never* wrong."

"I know others do it so I figured it would be OK."

"I'm *always* blamed."

Escaping/ Fantasy: Tendency to retreat into fantasy in order to resolve inner and outer conflicts.

"I hoped it would make me feel better."

"I didn't think I would get____." (Fill in the blank: arrested, sick, caught, hurt, etc.)

Your Primary Thinking Error

Even though we might use many thinking errors over time, sometimes one constant theme may be present throughout our thinking errors. We label this theme the "primary thinking error." It is often the foundation of how we make sense of the world. It is the thought that we first use to interpret any situation. The less information we have about a situation in real time, the more likely we are to base our assessment on our primary thinking error. As ingrained as this pattern of thinking is in our life, it is very difficult to recognize. In our earlier example, the people of Oz forgot they wore green colored glasses. They didn't recognize that their world looked green because that was the way their world had always looked to them. When everything is always green, we stop being aware of the green. Similarly, our primary thinking errors drive our behavior, making people and situations seem a certain way to us, yet like the green for the people of Oz, our primary thinking is hidden from us. We don't recognize it and we don't think about it.

Often it is the primary thinking error that drives our behavior. For example, if your primary thinking error is "I don't fit in," you might look for ways to use this thought of not fitting in to justify your behaviors. You might go online for a sexual chat because you avoid the risk of being rejected. If you're in a situation where you do feel rejected, you look at it as further proof of how you don't fit in. As a result, you constantly worry about not fitting in, and you look for that perfect situation where you don't have to worry about the possibility of not fitting in. It gets exhausting!

Identifying Your Primary Thinking Error

To identify your primary thinking error, complete the following exercise, listing the thoughts that come to mind. Don't analyze too much.

- Review the examples of Frequent Thinking Errors above. Which thinking errors, in relation to others, elicit the most intense reaction from you? It might be the ones where you say, "I say this often" or those where you say, "That is NOT me...no way." If any of the thinking error examples elicit a reaction, add it to the list of possibilities.

- Look at an incident where you acted-out. As you complete a behavioral analysis (see page 71), track the thoughts backward. We use the idea of dominos as an example. Think of a thought as a domino. Each domino's fall is triggered by the fall of the domino before it, and *that* domino's fall was triggered by the fall of the domino that preceded it, and the fall of all the dominoes can be traced down the line to the very first domino. In the same way, a thought is triggered by a preceding thought, and *that* thought was triggered by the thought that preceded it, all the way back to the initial thought. If we can trace our thoughts back to one "initial thought," we could find our primary thinking error.

- What life events, big or small, trigger the strongest reaction? Before you react, identify the internal conversation or thoughts you are having. What is the assumption you have about what happened or what you think the other person or persons involved did or said?

- Look back over times in your life when things did not go the way you wanted. These could be what you consider "big" things (such as losing a job, being called into the boss' office) or "small" things (such as plans with a friend falling through). What do you say to yourself to make sense of the situation? What might be your fear in these situations?

- When you look at your list of thoughts, restate them in a simple way. We encourage our clients to rephrase the thought as a six- or seven-year-old might phrase them. Here are some examples of primary thinking errors:

  - "It's my fault."
  - "I can't do it."
  - "It doesn't matter."
  - "Why try?"
  - "This won't work."
  - "You can't make me."
  - "I can do what I want."
  - "I don't fit in."
  - "Nobody wants me."
  - "I don't know."

It is important to emphasize that we are looking for a "thought" and not a feeling. If you identify a feeling in the process, ask yourself "Why do I feel this? What is the thought that creates that feeling?" Too often people will say, "I'm bad" or "I'm not good enough." Our response is to ask, *Why* do you feel that?"

These exercises are simply tools to help you pinpoint your primary thinking error. If you can't pinpoint it at this point, that's OK. You might be able to identify it later on as you start to look at incidents as they occur in real time.

As difficult as it is to identify the primary thinking error, the reward for identifying and recognizing it is amazing. Consider the reality that you cannot break a bad habit if you do not know you are engaging in a bad habit. In golf, for example, coaches often help you "unlearn" bad habits you picked up along the way. So it is with the primary thinking error. It is a habitual way of thinking. When we recognize our primary thinking error, new opportunities become possible. Part of freedom is the ability to do whatever we want to do, but another part of it is being able to step out of bad patterns and choose the direction in which we want to go. As you recognize how often you use the primary thinking error, you can make a different choice toward something else that is more important. "Mindfulness" is the process of becoming aware of the "here and now." Start to increase your mindfulness of your current thoughts

- If you have any emotional reaction, identify the thoughts associated with the reaction.

- Complete exercises #1-5 above under the subsection "Identifying Your Primary Thinking Error." Summarize any common themes here.

- Start to examine patterns of thinking that appear to be present in your life. What themes appear to be present at this point?

- Identify 3-5 thinking errors you use in your life.

- Review the section above on the psychology of the Internet. What role do you think the psychology of the Internet plays in the development and nature of your thinking errors.

- Review the list of thinking errors with your support network. Which thinking errors do they suggest might be consistently present?

- What are your initial plans to help you cope with these thinking errors?

Summary of Your Current Thinking Errors

Summarize the top 3 thinking errors so far. Identify 1-2 plans to start coping with these thinking errors. Return to the list and update as necessary.

1. _____

My plans for coping:

2. _____

My plans for coping:

3. _____

My plans for coping:

Feeling Triggers

A major factor in the acting-out cycle is the presence of a feeling trigger. As we said earlier, we agree with clients who say, "I don't know what I'm feeling" at the beginning of the therapy process. The growth process is about learning to identify and understand the feelings.

Major Feeling Triggers

Abandoned	Cheated	Envious	Jubilant	Reluctant
Accepted	Cheerful	Exasperated	Let down	Remorseful
Afraid	Confident	Excited	Lonely	Resentful
Alone	Courageous	Exhilarated	Merry	Resigned
Amazed	Cowardly	Fearful	Miserable	Sad
Ambivalent	Disappointed	Flighty	Mortified	Secure
Angry	Discontent	Free	Murderous	Selfish
Annoyed	Discouraged	Frightened	Nervous	Self-pity
Anxious	Dissatisfied	Frustrated	Numb	Shocked
Apathetic	Distressed	Glad	Overcome	Stunned
Apprehensive	Drained	Humble	Overjoyed	Surprised
Ashamed	Eager	Humiliated	Overwhelmed	Thrilled
Awe	Ecstatic	Hurt	Peaceful	Tired
Brave	Embarrassed	Indignant	Panicked	Triumphant
Calm	Empathy	Irritated	Pity	Uneasy
Careful	Empty	Jealous	Regretful	Unworthy
Caring	Encouraged	Jolly	Rejected	Vengeful
Cautious	Energized	Joyful	Relief	Wary
			Relieved	Weary

Identifying feelings is more difficult than most people realize. To that goal, the process is designed to help you increase your awareness. As you sit down before the computer, ask yourself, "What am I feeling?" Other strategies include asking, what would others be feeling? Am I feeling this? Or, "What feeling might I guess that I'm having? In both of these situations, end with confirming whether or not this feeling is present. It is important to remember that feelings are based on thoughts and the interpretation of the world around you. You might also ask, "What am I thinking?" and as a result, "How do I feel" given that I'm thinking this.

Above is a list of feelings that many people highlight as contributing to their Internet use. Notice that both positive and negative feelings are associated with the cycle. Keep in mind that feeling confident may lead to feelings of overconfidence, where you then place yourself at risk for an acting-out encounter. Another feeling might be anger or hurt. In some circumstances, some clients have reported they acted-out sexually as a way to get back at their partners. Review the list of feelings as they relate to the acting-out cycle.

Assignment

- Identify 3-5 feeling triggers you have in your life.

- Review the list of feeling triggers with your support network. Which feeling triggers do they suggest might be consistently present?

- What role do you think the psychology of the Internet plays in the development and nature of your feeling triggers?

Summary of Your Current Feeling Triggers

Summarize the top 3 feeling triggers so far. Identify 1-2 plans to start coping with these feeling triggers. Return to the list and update as necessary.

1. _____

My plans for coping:

2. _____

My plans for coping:

3. _____

My plans for coping:

High-Risk Situations

The next component in the acting-out cycle is high-risk situations. This is the easiest component to identify and the easiest component to create prevention plans for. Identifying and creating prevention plans for high-risk situations are very important, but they do not, alone, reduce sexual compulsivity. Underlying issues (such as thoughts/thinking errors and feeing triggers) must be addressed, or you will be able to easily circumvent structural interventions. The "structural interventions" (see below) are at best, speed bumps. They won't completely stop you from acting-out.

A high-risk situation is the setting in which acting-out behavior occurs. Picture yourself engaging in acting-out behavior, as though you were pictured in a photograph. What is going on in the photograph? Ask your self the classic questions, "Who," "What," "Where," "When," and "How" ("Why?" is used more in identifying thinking errors than in identifying high-risk situations) – these are the tools for identifying high-risk situations:

- "What was I doing right before?"
- "What was going on?"
- "Where was I?"
- "Who was with me?"
- "When did it happen?"
- "How did it happen?"

Some examples of high-risk situations are:

- "I was home alone."
- "I was surfing the Internet for work."
- "I was bored and surfing the Internet."
- "I had no reason to be online, I was just hanging out there."
- "I had a fight with my partner and decided to chill out by going online."
- "I was fired and feeling very worthless."

Developing a prevention plan for avoiding high-risk situations is simply a matter of creating a structural intervention that will get in the way or remove the high-risk situation. For example, if surfing the Internet is a trigger for you, possible structural interventions could be installing an Internet blocker or Internet tracker, having someone watch over you, or simply not having your house connected to the Internet. Avoiding high-risk situation is a first step in getting your online sexual behavior under control.

Assignment

- Identify 3-5 high-risk situations in your life.

- What role do you think the psychology of the Internet plays in the development and nature of your high-risk situations?

• Review the list of high-risk situations with your support network. Which high-risk situations do they suggest might be consistently present?

Summary of Your Current High-Risk Situations

Summarize the top 3 high-risk situations so far. Identify 1-2 plans to start coping with these high-risk situations. Return to the list and update as necessary.

1. _____

My plans for coping:

2. _____

My plans for coping:

3. _____

My plans for coping:

Payoffs—Why Have Sex?

Interrupting the acting-out cycle requires awareness of the payoffs for online sexual behavior. This is essentially answering the question, "Why go online?"

While the reasons for engaging in online sex may vary, it is important for you to uncover some of the reasons and payoffs that are important to you. ALL behavior is goal focused. Your online behavior is seeking some type of payoff.

Although payoffs are always present, awareness of these payoffs varies. Some payoffs are direct: "I find someone to hook-up with and have sex." Some of these payoffs are "hopes" that something will happen: "If an attractive person says 'yes', I'll be OK." In some circumstances, the reasons for online sexual behavior highlight clinical issues (depression), or patterns of the acting out cycle that you need to address. This is much more difficult than you may think. To put this in perspective, a recent journal article identified 237 reasons a person has sex separated into 13 factors.[4] As you review your online sexual behavior, consider the following:

- Physical reasons for sex:
  - Stress Reduction. "I am at work, and this gives me a distraction."
  - Pleasure. "Sex is fun." "Having an orgasm is fun."
  - Physical Desirability. "I want that person." "That person wants me."
  - Experience Seeking. "I'm bored and don't have anything to do." "I can do something online that I wouldn't do in person."

- Goal attainment for sex:
  - Resources. "I will get money/drugs."
  - Social Status. "My reputation will get better." "No body will know."
  - Revenge. "I will make that other person mad."
  - Utilitarian. "I will get a raise/promotion."

- Emotional reasons for online sexual behavior:
  - Love and Commitment. "I love you." "I'm scared of my partner."
  - Expression of Feelings. "I'm sorry." "I'm mad at my partner"

- Insecurity reasons for sex:
  - Self-Esteem Boost. "Someone wants me, I feel better."
  - Duty/Pressure. "My partner won't do what I want."
  - Mate Guarding. "I can't have sex with my partner, so I'll go online instead."

Levels of Payoff

We think about three different types of payoffs: Primary, Secondary, and Indirect. Primary payoffs roughly (but not always) parallel biological or immediate emotional needs. These are often the focus of the behavior. Consider the following examples"

It's been a long, hard day at work. I think I earned a break. I go online for stress release. While online, I start chatting with someone who wants to hook-up. I have great sex, feel great and get even more of a sense of relief from the stress. But I also feel shameful and guilty which reinforces why I need to work so hard to get a sense of affirmation thereby causing the stress. Additional examples of primary payoffs include:

- Great Sex.
- Sense of connection/intimacy.
- Finding things online that I can't find in person.
- Stress Reduction.

Secondary payoffs are pleasant outcomes of the behavior. While they aren't the first goal, the outcome also is a pleasant payoff:

I realize I may be attracted to someone of the same-gender (gay/bi/lesbian). I'm scared of meeting people, or others finding out so I go online. This way I avoid the rejection of others; a preferable outcome versus my parents or friends finding out.

I'm horny, and my partner doesn't want sex. I go online to look at sexually explicit material. While surfing, I go to a chat room and start to look at the pictures of other people and start chatting/video cam.

Examples of secondary payoffs might be:

- Sense of affirmation.
- Addresses boredom with something to do.
- I get to be someone I'm not in real life.
- No one will find out.
- Not alone for an evening.

Indirect payoffs are very subtle and complex to identify. They may or may not be present all the time. Sometimes the negative consequence is actually what we are seeking. We find that some people will actually sabotage their goals out of a fear of success. These individuals might have a high level of shame, such that the only sense of any accomplishment comes through getting in the way of their own progress.

Examples of indirect payoffs include the following:

- Reaffirms the negative feelings I have about myself.
- I can justify how much I work to make up for the negative feelings.

Notice that what is a payoff depends on the person. While some payoffs may appear similar across individuals, each person has their own unique pattern of payoffs. Review your sexual timeline and history and times where you acted-out. Examine which reasons for sexual behavior may be relevant. As you reflect on the reasons, examine your thoughts and assumptions. If, for example, a reason for sexual behavior is to increase self-esteem, examine the thoughts and feelings associated with the low esteem.

Assignment

- Review your timeline. Identify the payoffs for your most recent acting-out encounter. Pay attention to both the primary and secondary payoffs and the indirect payoffs. Pick another acting-out encounter and repeat.

- Analyze the timeline for the possible payoffs listed above.

- Share these with your support network. Do they agree? Disagree? Why? Which payoffs do they suggest might be present?

Summary of Your Current Payoffs for Sexual Behavior

Summarize the top 3 payoffs so far. Identify 1-2 plans to start coping with these payoffs. Return to the list and update as necessary.

1. _____

My plans for coping:

2. _____

My plans for coping:

3. _____

My plans for coping:

Acting-out and Other Compulsive Behaviors

When examining the acting-out cycle, it is important to recognize related behaviors. Often the online sexual behavior is not the first level of acting-out, but rather the culmination of a number of behavior cycles. A number of classic forms of acting-out are briefly examined. Should you find that some of these forms are relevant, please work with your therapist and support network.

Sexual Avoidance

"How can I have a sex problem if I do not have sex?" Thoughts and feelings of shame, fear, and hopelessness can cause a person to avoid sexual contact. Sexual avoidance describes the state of depriving oneself of sex. One of the more difficult aspects of sexual avoidance is recognizing the problem. People easily know when they are not having sex, but they might not recognize that not having sex can mean they are out of control – just as having sex can mean they are out of control. Sexual avoidance, or "sexual anorexia," is a less recognized – and as a result less treated–condition. Understanding the motivating factor underlying the lack sex is what is important. The lack of sex is not important in itself. Often the underlying cause for sexual avoidance is similar to the cause for sexual compulsivity. It is important for you to assess the presence of sexual avoidance in addition to the presence of sexual compulsivity.

Chemical Dependency

Chemical dependency is a treatment issue in and of itself. If you struggle with chemical use we cannot overstate the importance of addressing this issue. The purpose of this section is to help you recognize any connections between your sexual behavior and chemical dependency by reviewing some of the indicators of chemical dependency, providing a screening tool, and then highlighting possible relationships between chemical dependency and sexual behavior. If appropriate, include chemical use in your timeline. When clinicians interview people for indicators of chemical dependency, they typically look for the following signs:[5]

- Problems completing responsibilities at work, school or home as a result of chemical use.
- Using chemicals when it is physically hazardous (such as driving a car).
- Recurrent substance-related legal problems.
- Continued substance use despite having persistent consequences.
- Tolerance, as defined by either of the following: (a) a need for markedly increased amounts of the substance to achieve intoxication or the desired effect or (b) markedly diminished effect with continued use of the same amount of the substance.
- Withdrawal, as manifested by either of the following: (a) the characteristic withdrawal syndrome for the substance or (b) the same (or closely related) substance is taken to relieve or avoid withdrawal symptoms.
- The substance is often taken in larger amounts or over a longer period than intended.

- There is a persistent desire or unsuccessful effort to cut down or control substance use.
- A great deal of time is spent in activities necessary to obtain the substance, use the substance or recover from its effects.
- Important social, occupational or recreational activities are given up or reduced because of substance use.
- The substance use is continued despite knowledge of having a persistent physical or psychological problem that is likely to have been caused or exacerbated by the substance.

There is a distinction between chemical use, chemical abuse and chemical dependency. For example, you might drink alcohol and find there's nothing wrong with doing so. However, there might be times when you have engaged in unhealthy, risky or unwise behaviors while drinking. If this happens rarely, this might qualify for "chemical abuse." If you're level of use is higher, and you engage in a number of risky behaviors, or if the number of symptoms is higher, this might qualify as "chemical dependency."

It is important for you to identify your level of use, so that treatment options can be determined. The more severe the level of use, the more intensive the treatment option will need to be. A helpful tool is the classic alcohol-screening "CAGE" questionnaire derived from the following four questions:

- Have you ever felt you ought to *cut* down on your drinking?
- Have people *annoyed* you by criticizing your drinking?
- Have you ever felt bad or *Guilty* about your drinking?
- Have you ever had a drink first thing in the morning to steady your nerves or get rid of a hangover (*Eye-opener*)?

Give yourself one point for each "yes" answer. A total score of two or more is generally considered clinically significant and warrants further assessment.[6] A similar drug screen questionnaire can be found at the following link: http://counsellingresource.com/quizzes/drug-abuse/index.html. Both screening tests are provided for your information. If your scores are higher, we strongly recommend you seek additional assessment and treatment if necessary.

Eating Disorders

When the topic of eating disorders is raised, the person that often comes to mind is an adolescent female or young woman throwing up to reduce her weight because of bad body image. Although women account for the majority of eating disorders, the number of men with eating disorders is growing. Among gay men, the percentage is even higher.

Typically, eating disorders fall into three conditions: Anorexia Nervosa, Bulimia Nervosa and Eating Disorder, Not Otherwise Specified. Anorexia Nervosa is typically exhibited through the failure to eat or maintain proper nutrition. Bulimia Nervosa is typically exhibited through purging behaviors such as throwing up or laxative use. Most often, however, you will not find a person with an either/or diagnosis, hence the combined diagnosis of Eating Disorder, Not Otherwise Specified, which is sort of a catchall diagnosis. Symptoms of an eating disorder include:

- Significant changes in weight.
- Eating more than a typical person does in a typical meal.
- Constantly thinking about food.
- Constantly thinking about body image.
- Constantly thinking "I'm fat."
- Purging after eating.
- Over-exercising.
- Excessive use of laxatives.

Although it is difficult to accurately diagnose eating disorders, there are assessment tools. One researcher identified four questions that may be helpful. If you answer "yes" to three of the questions, she recommends you seek further assessment. [7]

- Do you worry you have lost control over how much you eat?
- Do you make yourself sick when you feel uncomfortably full?
- Do you currently suffer with, or have you ever suffered in the past, from an eating disorder?
- Do you ever eat in secret?

Eating Disorders are included in this workbook because it is necessary to review how your eating behaviors are associated with your sexual behaviors. Part of addressing eating disorders will also require you to address the questions of body image. Review your online sex history and the timeline. Is there any correlation between your sexual behavior, frequency, thoughts and feelings and your eating behaviors or body image? Might an eating disorder episode precede or follow sexual behaviors? Do sexual behaviors trigger shame, which is transferred to eating behaviors?

Gambling

Another area of concern for some individuals is their gambling behavior. The question is to assess any relationship between gambling behaviors as a reaction to sexuality or sexuality as a reaction to gambling. Review the referenced South Oaks Gambling Screen located at: http://www.addictionrecov.org/southoak.htm. Review your sexual timeline. Is there any relationship between your sexual behavior and gambling behaviors?

Spending

Spending behavior can be related to sexual behavior. Like many of the similar cross-compulsive behaviors, each of these issues may require treatment in its own right. Some behaviors that suggest that spending is compulsive:

- Shopping or spending money as a result of feeling disappointed, angry or scared.
- Shopping or spending habits are causing emotional distress.
- Arguing with others about your shopping or spending habits.
- Feeling lost without credit cards.
- Buying items on credit that you aren't able to buy with cash.
- Feeling a rush of euphoria and anxiety when spending money.
- Feeling guilty, ashamed, embarrassed or confused after shopping or spending.
- Lying to others about your purchases or spending.
- Thinking excessively about money.
- Spending a lot of time juggling accounts or bills to accommodate spending.

Another researcher highlights five factors that may suggest compulsive spending behaviors.[8] These factors are:

- A tendency to shop and spend in binges or "buying episodes."
- A preoccupation, compulsion, and impulsiveness in shopping and spending patterns.
- Compulsive spending because the person enjoys the shopping and spending activity.
- Significant life-functioning issues surrounding and resulting from his or her shopping and spending behavior.
- Feelings of remorse, regret, and shame.

As you examine your spending behavior, review the questions above. Are you engaging in compulsive spending behaviors? Does compulsive spending precede sexual behavior? Might compulsive sexual behavior be an attempt to "cope" with spending behavior (i.e., does spending overcome feelings of guilt or shame)? Are you spending money to buy love or sex?

Compulsive Working

Compulsive working can contribute to problematic online sexual behaviors. This is also difficult to assess because our culture rewards hard workers. As with many of the compulsive behaviors, the degree of the problem is often on a continuum of severity. This topic is provided here to jumpstart your treatment process in order to review how work and sexual behaviors overlap. In some cases, the reality is that we simply don't recognize the compulsive patterns. There is not much academic research in the area. Here is a website addressing some basic questions for your consideration: http://www.hinduonnet.com/jobs/0011/05080033.htm

- Do you treat your home as your second office, and do you regularly take work home?
- Do you use hard work to justify your online behaviors?
- Do you take office work with you on a vacation or take smart devices, such as a laptop, a cell phone or a pager to keep in touch with your work life?
- Do you prefer being isolated and buried in your work, shunning all forms of social activity? Do you brush social activity aside as "trivial?"
- Do you not enjoy the returns of hard work (professional success, money) because you are too busy working?
- Are you physically run down because of overwork and stress, and you cannot be bothered?

Applying the concepts of the acting-out cycle, examine the motivations behind your work behaviors by looking at the thoughts and feelings you have before, during or after work. Your reaction to work can trigger thinking errors you may use to justify your sexual behavior. You might use sexual behavior to help escape work, or use hard work as justification for a sexual contact.

Assignment

Review your sex history and timeline. Identify other forms of acting-out from the discussion and lists above. What are your plans to address these issues?

Putting it all Together — Behavioral Analysis

Clients often report they don't know why they did what they did. And to a large degree, we believe them. We often challenge clients by asking them to list the steps necessary to drive a car. As they do, we playfully trip them up by asking questions about this or that. What they come to realize is that driving a car is a remarkably complex task that calls for multiple thought processes requiring you to pay attention to details. In psychology, this term is called "automaticity," the ability to complete complex behaviors without active cognitive thinking – like a habit. Much of the ritual in Internet sexual compulsivity is automatic. People fall into a trance, and simply don't know why they are doing what they are doing. A helpful tool in identifying thinking errors, feeling triggers and high-risk situations is the completion of a behavioral analysis. This is a step-by-step examination of what happens in an acting-out experience. The goal is to help you identify additional relevant issues, so you should examine all details, no matter how small you think they are. The behavioral analysis is a way to slow down and uncover the contributing factors. In the process of completing the analysis, you will identify a number of places to intervene and interrupt the cycle.

- You will learn to recognize and then contradict thinking errors. Challenging negative thinking through corrected thoughts or using affirmations (if you are familiar with the 12-step tradition) is a start.

- You will be able to address your feelings. Identifying ways you can connect with others in a healthy way, for example, allows you to help address feelings of loneliness. If your sadness and depression are significant and long lasting, medications or therapy might be helpful.
- High-risk situations are recognizable. Too much free time can make you vulnerable to a high-risk situation. Finding ways to engage in healthy fun is another way to intervene in the cycle.

In each of the behavioral analyses, we talk about an escalating pattern of behaviors that sets the stage for the next trip through the cycle. When working with clients, we call these trips "micro-cycles," because you may experience multiple trips through the cycle within a given time period. The example below highlights multiple ways you may have failed to cope with the setups throughout a given time period. The key then is to identify ways you can interrupt any and all of the various parts of the cycle.

Assignment

Using the template below, complete a behavioral analysis of a recent online sexual acting out experience. Which thinking errors (see page 48), feeling triggers (see page 57), high-risk situations (see page 59) and payoffs (see page 61) can you identify? Update your current lists, as appropriate.

Instructions

To complete the analysis, it may be helpful to work backwards. Start with the acting-out incident. Answer the question "What happened?" Then ask, "What happened right before that" and so on. Stay focused on what happened while you work backward. Don't give up to early, but you can always add more if you remember parts of the cycle. It's like tracing the last domino's fall back to the first domino. Once you have a good start at what happened, complete the other columns by adding the corresponding thinking errors/thoughts, feeling triggers and high-risk settings. Try to fill each column, but if you can't you can always come back to it. At the end of the process, summarize the behavioral analysis. Every item in the analysis becomes a place to develop an intervention plan.

—START HERE— What happened? Include Payoffs or Consequences	THOUGHTS What was I thinking? What reason did I use?	FEELINGS What was I feeling?	HIGH-RISK SITUATIONS When, where, who, what?
I spend 3 hours online looking at porn and masturbating	I did it again.	Shame. Hopelessness.	Isolation. Avoid my support network. Late night No support
I went to a porn site	Just visiting one site is ok, I won't stay here long. It is only a couple of pics	Justified, entitled	No monitoring, no supervision
Started surfing with no purpose	I deserve a little down time	Bored	
I was checking my email	I have to see what else needs to be done on the project.	Lonely, tired, sad.	Working too late Using work to give me an excuse to use the Internet "Work-aholic"
I was heading to bed	Can't talk to anyone. I'm alone. No one cares	Sad, depressed, lonely, tired.	Isolation. Tired Overworked
I had a fight	I can't do anything right. My partner doesn't understand. It's my fault	Fear, sadness, shame, guilt.	Seeing someone angry. Conflict Lack of assertive skills

The Process of Change and the Role of Relapse

In the field of online sexual compulsivity treatment, addressing the reality of a relapse is important. It is highly probably that you will experience some type of relapse around your high-risk situations, feeling triggers or thinking errors. You will move into a realm of acting out behaviors somewhere in your process. Why? Most likely because you're HUMAN! Being human acknowledges that perfection is not possible. Here are a few suggestions to help you address a sexual health relapse.

In the process of moving toward sexual health, to assume that you will never make a mistake sets you up for the cycle of shame and guilt that is probably a big part of your cycle at this point. Now, this doesn't mean being human is permission to relapse (nice thinking error), but it does provide a starting point toward self-forgiveness.

Depending on the circumstances, the ease with which relapses occur in the online world is shocking. Relapse can be a learning process (versus a source of guilt). By examining the relapse, you can uncover new factors associated with your acting out cycle as well as set up plans to address these factors. In many cases, the relapse can help prioritize treatment issues.

The degree of relapse can be a sign of progress. Often what happens is that the frequency and/or intensity of acting out decreases. Rather than hooking up with someone via a website, the behavior this time might be limited to viewing sexually explicit material. While still something to be addressed, this is progress. (For a more formal discussion, search out the term harm-reduction.)

"Telling on yourself" when a small or large relapse occurs is a reflection of the treatment progress. By using your support network, you demonstrate the skills to move toward health. The amount of disclosure to your primary network is a measure of your progress. Your ability to learn from the relapse is also a measure of your progress.

The biggest thing to recognize is that it is not the relapse that is important; it is what you do with the relapse. Do you take responsibility? Do you examine the response to learn why it occurred? Do you tell your therapist and someone in your support network? Do you makes changes to ensure it that it is less likely to happen again. A relapse can be a sign of progress especially when you own, it, examine it, tell someone, and make changes.

Assignment

Write out your plan on how you will handle the relapse when it happens. Share your plan with your therapist and/or support network.

Stage 2: Primary Treatment: Related Topics

Online Internet behavior doesn't happen out of the blue. It occurs in a context, and it is important that you understand that context. Stage 2 discusses the major issues related to online sexual compulsivity, issues that are identified through completing and reviewing the assignments from Stage 1. Specifically, these assignments include your sex history, timeline, Internet diaries, and any behavioral analyses. In Stage 2, you will begin to work on underlying issues. We provide assignments and resources for you. We recommend that you consider each topic, even if it appears that a particular topic does not apply to you. As you review the topics, ask yourself if you think you can address the issues on your own, or need professional help.

Depending on your current situation, you need to prioritize the topics. This process is known as "triage," a review and ranking of the issues, prioritizing and developing treatment plans for addressing the most important issues first. In other words, "first things first." Only you, in consultation with your support network, can prioritize the issues. It may not be wise to address the Internet sexual compulsivity behaviors at this time if other issues are more important. At the same time, if your sexual behavior contributes to the concerns, it may be even *more* important to address your sexual behavior issues.

In the list below are the topics in Stage 2. We've tried to be thorough, however we have no doubt you'll be able to add your own issues to the list. If something is relevant in your life, please add it to the list. The information in the workbook is a brief introduction to the topic; as you learn which topics are most important, work with your support network to obtain more information and support as needed. As you read the list, score each topic area on a four-point scale:

0   = Not a concern (e.g., "I was never abused as an adult or growing up").

1   = Minimal concern (e.g., "I feel anxious only at certain times; I do not think it is connected to my behaviors at this time").

2   = Significant concern (e.g., My sex life is so bad, I can only get it through the Internet.")

3   = Vital concern (e.g., "I'm so depressed I can't seem to do anything." "My relationship is in danger of ending because of my behaviors").

Topic	Severity 0. Not a concern 1. Minimal Concern 2. Significant Concern 3. Vital Concern	Final Rank
Culture and Stereotypes, see page 77		
Feelings of Shame and Guilt, see page 84		
Sexual Identity and Sexual Orientation, see page 87		
Sexual Functioning, see page 94		
Mental Health Factors, see page 106		
Types and Impact of Abuse, see page 115		
Feelings of Grief, see page 122		
Feelings of Anger, see page 126		
Body Image, see page 129		
Fantasy and Masturbation, see page 133		
Sexually Explicit Material, see page 141		
Positive Sexuality, see page 144		
Assertive Communication, see page 145		
Boundaries, see page 148		
Sexual Behavior and Expression, see page 151		
Healthy Sexual Behaviors, see page 153		
Desire for Intimacy, see page 158		
Touch/Physical Intimacy, see page 164		
Dating and Sexual Health, see page 167		
Healing from Past Relationships, see page 171		
Steps in Building the Sexual Relationship, page 173		
Types of Relationships, see page 175		
Disclosure to Partners, see page 180		
Spirituality, Values and Sexual Health, page 185		
Anything else on your list		

After you have scored the topics, go back and rank the areas that hold the most importance, sorting the "3's," "2's" and "1's" in an order that makes sense to you. This list will serve as a tentative plan to help pinpoint the topics you should address first in your treatment process.

Culture and Stereotypes

You are a product of the multiple cultures to which you belong (such as racial, ethnic, religious and age), and these cultures are in a constant tug-of-war, shaping your thoughts, beliefs, values, behaviors, wants and desires – including your sexual values and behaviors. In this section, we look at a variety of cultures as they shape our lives. We examine the cultures to which you might belong, and we also take a special look at the culture and components of sexual identity. The concept of online culture is relatively new and as a result it is not as well researched as other cultures.

Your Cultures and Stereotypes

We each belong to multiple cultures, and the various cultures to which we belong help us understand and make sense of the world. Everything we know is taught to us through these cultures. Much of what we see as sexually arousing is defined by the cultures to which we belong — such as family, race, gender, religious connection, sexual identity or nationality — and the things that sexually arouse us can change over time. These cultures shape sexual behaviors, values and identity. Improving your sexual health requires that you increase your awareness of your cultural values. It is important for you to understand all of the cultures to which you belong and how they influence your thoughts, beliefs and expectations. Shorthand ways of understanding the world are labeled as stereotypes. Our discussion is designed to help you identify and challenge some stereotypes

The various cultures to which we belong may conflict with one another. For example, in Latino culture, "machismo" (loosely understood as hyper-masculinity) is a typical male stereotype, and it is considered wrong for a man to show any weakness or feminine characteristics. If a man who belongs to the Latino culture wants to acknowledge that he is attracted to other men, then the two cultures are in conflict. A cyber example is becoming aware of a same-sex attraction as you surf the net, which conflicts with your relationship status in the offline world as well as your religious culture. Resolving such conflicts is crucial to increasing your personal sexual health. Some people resolve such conflicts by rejecting parts of their heritage; others work toward changing the culture they came from. They key is for you to integrate the cultures to which you belong within your overall identity.

Think about how you use the Internet in responding to or otherwise addressing cultural issues. For example, someone with a restrictive religious culture might use the Internet, since "it isn't really cheating." Someone else might use it to answer questions about sexual orientation, since it doesn't require disclosure.

Assignment

Identify the various cultures to which you belong. Identify two sexual beliefs you learned from each culture. Consider the following types of cultures:

Racial Culture

Racial Culture is often used synonymously with "skin color." (This usage is limiting, but we use it here for our general discussion.) It is important to see how your thoughts are shaped by assumptions about race.

Please complete the following sentences:

I belong to the_____ racial culture. Two sexual beliefs I learned are:

1.

2.

Ethnic / Nationality Culture

For our purposes, we use this term describe national origin. Are you from Poland, Indonesia, or Senegal? Some ethnic cultures cross over national boundaries. And many countries have multiple ethnic groups.

Please complete the following sentences:

I belong to the_____ culture. Two sexual beliefs I learned are:

1.

2.

Religious Culture

This refers to the shared beliefs regarding God and spirituality. In the United States, these beliefs might include (among others) Judeo-Christian, Islamic or Atheistic beliefs, but even within each religious tradition are multiple sub-cultures that shape sexual values.

Please complete the following sentences:

I belong to the_____ culture. Two sexual beliefs I learned are:

1.

2.

Age

The era in which we grew up and the generation to which we belong influence our sexual views. Someone who grew up in the 1930's views sexuality differently from someone who grew up in the 1970's. This results in different values that shape sexuality.

Please complete the following sentences:

I belong to the_____ culture. Two sexual beliefs I learned are:

1.

2.

Gender and Sexual Orientation

We'll look at sexual identity in detail (see page 87), but for now, let's say sexual identity includes our gender (male/female), and sexual orientation (gay/straight/bi). There are numerous stereotypes regarding sexual identity. Each stereotype shapes our understanding of sexuality.

Please complete the following sentences:

I belong to the (male/female/trans)_____ culture. Two sexual beliefs I learned are:

1.

2.

I identify as (gay/bi/straight)_____. Two sexual beliefs I learned are:

1.

2.

Socioeconomic Status

Socioeconomic status means your level of wealth and your standard of living. Socioeconomic status shapes your view of sexuality. (For example, sharing a bed with a parent takes on a new meaning if you have a one-room house.) Please complete the following sentences, indicating whether you belong to a wealthy, middle class or poor socioeconomic culture.

Please complete the following sentences:

I belong to the_____ culture. Two sexual beliefs I learned are:

1.

2.

Disability Status

Disability refers to mental, physical, or emotional disabilities. Some may occur at birth (mental handicap), or be acquired (illnesses). There are beliefs based on disability.

Please complete the following sentences:

I belong to the (disabled_____) (non-disabled_____) culture. Two sexual beliefs I learned are:

1.

2.

Geographic Status

Geographic status can be national or regional. Within the United States, for example, there are differences in sexual values based on region – northern, southern, eastern, and western. Please complete the following sentences:

I belong to the_____ culture.

Two sexual beliefs I learned are:

1.

2.

Online Cyber Culture

This refers to the thoughts you have about online sexual behaviors.

Please complete the following sentences:

Two sexual beliefs I learned are:

1.

2.

Assignment

• Which cultural messages are unhelpful to you?

• Which cultural messages are helpful to you?

• Each of us is a product of the many cultures to which we belong. What values from different cultures are in conflict? How do you resolve such conflicts?

- How have you used the Internet to respond to the cultural messages?

After reviewing your answers, think about what you've learned about yourself or others based on this assignment. How have these beliefs shaped your online sexual behavior? Share with your support team. Be sure to challenge some of the assumptions you listed.

Feelings of Shame and Guilt

By definition, culture is where we learn shame and guilt. Many people struggle with shaming messages about sexuality. It is important to understand the difference between the two. Below we highlight our understanding of the basic differences between shame and guilt. Consider how shame and guilt relate to your online sexual behavior.

Shame

Shame is a feeling based on a thought that as a person, you are bad, worthless, unforgiveable, and defective. Shame is *person focused*. ("I am a bad person.") The associated thought is that everyone knows and rejects you. There is a belief that nothing can fix the shame, that you will never be able to get better, or that you cannot find redemption. Associated feelings of shame are despair, hopelessness, loneliness, embarrassment and humiliation. When people have feelings of shame, their behaviors often hurt both themselves and others. Shame-based behaviors can include a lack of respect for themselves and others, justification for abuse toward themselves and others and lack of empathy for others. Often shame exists within a cognitive framework of perfectionism ("I can't make a mistake; it has to be perfect. All online sexual material is bad."). People who feel shame often focus on covering up, hiding and displaying a false front to mask their intense feelings. Because of shame, people will engage in behaviors to compensate in the hope that others will like them. People who feel shame lose a sense of boundaries in an attempt to cope. Some writers [9] distinguish between healthy and toxic shame. We believe that all shame is unhealthy, and that a person needs to distinguish between shame and guilt.

Guilt

Guilt is a feeling based on a thought that your behavior is wrong, bad, awful, terrible and hurtful. Guilt is the recognition that you violated your ethical values and morality. Guilt is *act focused*. ("I feel guilty when I have done something wrong.") When you feel guilty about something you have done, you do not have to feel shame. Because guilt is about your behavior, you usually can do something about it. You can apologize, forgive, learn, change, develop and grow in response to the guilt. You can set boundaries, repair the damage and rebuild relationships. Guilt is normal, appropriate and even healthy. Guilt is unhealthy when you feel an inappropriate amount of guilt, or when you feel guilty when you haven't done anything wrong. If these feelings are present, you are probably stuck in shame. We encourage our clients to feel guilty when the feeling is appropriate. In the context of sexual health, some behaviors are wrong and guilt is the recognition that you did something wrong (e.g., "I lied about what I did online").

You learn both shame and guilt from the same sources, including family of origin, religion, school, friends, government, and society. Learning the concept of responsibility is also a cultural process. A person learns responsibility through parenting, role modeling and holding others accountable for their behavior. The goal for individuals is to learn from their mistakes. In our society, shame is taught more often than responsibility. The phrase, *"Shame on you"* should be changed to *"Guilt on you."*

It is important to examine cultural sources of shame such as racism, sexism and heterosexism. Each of these forms of prejudice shows a negative judgment on entire groups. From these cultural sources of shame, individuals learn shame directly (overt) and indirectly (covert). Individuals are taught that being different is wrong. Shame is taught overtly when children are told they are bad, they're put down as worthless, or they're made fun of and teased cruelly. The difficulty with cyber behavior is that often seeking or using online material may be an attempt to cope with these larger negative judgments. People who violate the boundaries of others in emotional, psychological, physical and sexual ways teach shame. Covert shaming (such as a negative comments made about gay people in news media) can be difficult to recognize. It is based in poor education, poor modeling and unsupportive relationships.

Assignment

One assignment we sometimes give clients who are stuck in shame is to list 100, or even 500, shaming messages they tell themselves. Clients will often resist, but once the start they are amazed at how easy it is to identify the messages. The second part of the assignment is to challenge the underlying thinking errors that contribute to the shaming messages. Ask yourself the following questions:

- What shameful messages did you hear growing up?

- Who provided these messages?

- How do these messages impact you today?

- What shaming messages did you hear regarding sexuality?

- If part of a minority group (e.g., you're a woman, a person of color, a gay person, etc.), what shaming messages have you heard?

- What shaming messages do you experience now?

- How have you used the Internet to cope with shaming messages?

- What cybersex behaviors trigger feelings of shame?

- Now, repeat the same questions substituting the word *shame* with the word *guilt*.

Sexual Identity and Sexual Orientation

Sometimes the Internet is used as a place to gain information. In the realm of sexuality, identity is a-place individuals use to explore, connect, and understand given their fear and confusion about sexual identity. Before we get to sexual orientation, we first want to have a discussion of sexual identity in the broad sense.

Identity is a statement "this is who I am." In the process of clarifying this identity, individuals go through a process of sorting through life events, responding "like-me/not like me." This is an oversimplification, but identity development is the attempt to define and understand who we are. It is an interactive process that everyone goes through – often unconsciously – in understanding his or her sexual selves. Obviously, this process also occurs in the area of sexual orientation. The next section discusses the process of forming sexual identity and sexual orientation and the related tasks that need to be addressed. People use the two terms interchangeably, but they are in fact different. All messages of sexual identity are culturally informed. It is important to review how your sexual identity relates to your sexual health.

Four Components of Sexual Identity

Sexual identity is complex. Following are four components of sexual identity. Each component plays a role in your sexual identity.

Natal Sex

This refers to your biological makeup at birth. Often this refers to your sexual genitalia or your DNA makeup. Women have X-X chromosomes, while men have X-Y chromosomes. Most often this correlates to vaginal or penile genitalia.[10] Most of the time, identifying a person's genital sex is as simple as observing the baby when it's born. ("It's a *boy*!" or "It's a *girl*!")

Gender Identity

Gender Identity is the gender you feel you are. Most often this matches one's natal sex. "I have the genitalia of a female, and I feel female." When natal sex does not match Gender Identity (i.e., it is not congruent), the situation falls under the broad term "transgender." People who are transgender believe they are the opposite sex from their physical body. In such a situation, people may say they feel trapped in the wrong body. For example, a biological male believes he is female, or a biological female believes she is male. Identifying as transgender is not a psychosis or neurosis. If you believe that you are transgender, please seek help from a trained professional. It is a complex topic beyond the scope of this workbook.

Social Sex Roles

Easy to understand but often misunderstood, social sex roles refer to culturally defined behaviors based on one's gender. Typically, social sex roles are divided into masculine roles and feminine roles, but these roles may change over time, hence the potential for confusion. Social sex roles reflect what a man is "supposed to be like" or what a woman is a woman is "supposed to be like." Often, social sex roles are confused with sexual identity. For example, an effeminate male labeled as "gay." Common thoughts such as "All guys do it" or "Women aren't sexual" are thinking errors related to social sex roles. These are examples of how culture shapes our social sex roles.

Sexual Orientation

This is most often described as a same-sex attraction or a heterosexual attraction. Often people simply say, "I'm a gay man" or "I'm a lesbian woman" or "I'm a straight female." This concept is not necessarily clear-cut.

Sexual Orientation Explored

In the pre-Internet days, if a person wanted to gain information on sexual orientation, the few places to look were typically a dictionary or an encyclopedia article. The fear of asking a librarian for help was too much for many. Now, the Internet makes such information easily available. Much research has gone into understanding the causes of sexual orientation. Generally, the conclusion is that science just does not know.

> No single scientific theory about what causes sexual orientation has been suitably substantiated. Studies to associate sexual orientation with genetic, hormonal, and environmental factors have so far been inconclusive. Sexual orientation is no longer considered to be one's conscious individual preference or choice, but is instead thought to be formed by a complicated network of social, cultural, biological, economic, and political factors. *Sex Information and Educational Council of the US (SIECUS), 1993.*

There are a number of myths regarding the cause of a same-sex attraction. The research makes it clear that a history of sexual abuse does not cause a same-sex attraction. Same-sex orientation is not a psychopathology. Based on research showing no greater evidence of mental illness among individuals with same-sex attractions vs. those with an opposite-sex attraction, in 1973, the American Psychiatric Association removed homosexuality from its list of mental health disorders. An individual's sexual orientation also appears to stabilize over time. What might change, however, is one's acceptance of, or expression of, one's sexual orientation. All major health associations in the United States, including the American Psychiatric Association, the American Medical Association and the American Psychological Association, consider it unethical to attempt to change one's sexual orientation (known as the ex-gay movement or reparative therapy).

The "Kinsey Continuum" was an early attempt to understand sexual orientation and sought to rate one's *genital sexual behaviors* on a scale ranging from "exclusively heterosexual" to "exclusively homosexual." Adaptations of the continuum include "fantasy content" and "emotional relationships." Look at each topic to see where you fit on the continuum. With whom do you have sexual contact? What gender is in your fantasies? Who are your closest friends?

Adapted Kinsey Continuum

	0	1	2	3	4	5	6	
Exclusively Heterosexual							Exclusively Homosexual	

Stages of Identity Development

Many people who have a same-sex identity experience a process of moving toward a place of acceptance. We call this a "coming out process." Consider how your online sexual behavior might be related to this process. Vivian Cass presents one model of identity development that might be helpful in understanding a same-sex sexual identity. She hypothesizes six stages:

Stage 1 — Identity Confusion

Heterosexual identity is called into question with a person's increasing awareness of feelings of intimate and physical attraction toward others of the same sex. Individuals will start asking themselves the question "Could I be homosexual?" Gay and lesbian information or awareness on the Internet becomes personally relevant, and the heterosexual assumption begins to be undermined. You might actually start seeking out gay-lesbian content. At this stage, confusion is great and denial is usually the primary coping strategy.

Stage 2 — Identity Comparison

Individuals begin accepting the potential that homosexual feelings are a part of the self. The realization that "I might be homosexual" may cross your mind. Perhaps due to shame and guilt, the individual expresses a same-sex identity only online. The idea that "I may be bisexual" (which permits the potential for heterosexuality) can also be a manifestation of this stage. It is also at this level that the belief "This is a 'phase' I'm going through" may surface. These strategies reduce the incongruence between same-sex attractions and a view of one's self as heterosexual. The task at this stage of identity comparison, according to Cass, is to deal with social alienation as the individual becomes aware the individual's difference from larger society.

Stage 3 — Identity Tolerance

This is marked by statements such as, "I only look at gay stuff online, but I don't do anything with other people." Online chat may be a tool used at this stage. This declaration results in a sense of clarity for individuals, but it also results in a sense of separation from others, because the individuals recognize that they are "different." For individuals who experience a heightened need for peer approval and acceptance, this can be a difficult period. During this period, individuals often create a well-developed facade to "mask" and hide this part of them. Individuals often struggle with a constant need to hide their sexual orientation. Relationships are hurt, at least in the minds of the individuals, because of the secret identity. Positive experiences are crucial to developing a degree of self-acceptance during this period. Contacting other gay, lesbian and/or bisexual people becomes a more pressing issue to alleviate a sense of isolation and alienation. It also provides individuals with the experience of accepting their whole being, and not just their "mask."

Stage 4 — Identity Acceptance

Contact with other gay men and lesbian women increases. Finding other gay and lesbian persons is important. Although this was difficult for older generations, younger generations are often easily able to find support groups. Those individuals fortunate enough to have access to support groups or social events often experience a heightened sense of their identity and a sense of self-acceptance. There is a move away from hiding the identity to sharing their identity with people in their life. They can begin to address issues of "Who am I?" and "How do I fit in?"

Stages 5 and 6 — Identity Pride and Identity Synthesis

Individuals move from a "them and us" mentality into a realization and acceptance of the similarities between the heterosexual and homosexual worlds. Strong identification with the gay subculture and devaluation of heterosexuality and many of its institutions (Stage 5) give way to less rigid, polarizing views and more inclusive and cooperative behavior (Stage 6).

Men Who Have Sex with Men: Not All Gay-Sex is Gay

Not all men who have sex with men will identify as being gay. In many cases, we use the phrase "men who have sex with men" to focus on the behavior versus a label. Some of these men do not identify as gay because they are "in the closet" and in denial about their sexual orientation, attempting to minimize, avoid or deny their same-sex attractions. In some cases, men who have sex with men are truly not gay. For these men, having sex with another men results in minimal guilt, because they can say "I didn't have sex with another woman" or supports the flattering notion that they can find sexual partners easily. In some situations (prison, military or religious settings), the only available sexual partner is someone of the same gender (aka "situational homosexuality"). For this person, if both genders were available, he would choose the opposite gender. As a final example, the behavior may have occurred under the influence of alcohol or other chemicals.

While all of these examples show men engaging in sexual behavior with people of the same sex, their behaviors do not add up to a "gay identity." A great resource on this issue is at http://www.straightguise.com. Dr. Joe Kort has identified 12 types of same-sex behavior that may not be the result of a gay-identity. Unfortunately, there is limited similar research paralleling female same-sex behavior.

Bisexuality

In our opinion, bisexuality (a sexual orientation where a person is attracted to both men and women) is a true orientation. What makes understanding bisexuality difficult is that it is sometimes used to describe a transitory term in the coming-out process. This multiple uses of the term leads to confusion in the larger community that can make it harder for a person to clarify a bisexual orientation. A bisexual person has to cope with stereotypes from the straight community and also from the gay and lesbian communities. It is sometimes said that a bisexual has to "come out" twice, once in the straight community and a second time in the gay/lesbian community. As you examine your sexual identity, consider whether a bisexual orientation is related to your online sexual behavior.

Often, people think bisexuality is only about sex, but there are many variables to consider. Regarding sexual orientation, there are three variables: genital behavior, physical attraction, and emotional attraction. For instance, think about whom you connect with emotionally. Think about whom you are attracted to intellectually or socially. You might realize, "I may be attracted to men on a physical level, but I connect better with women on an emotional level." In thinking about these variables, you get the idea that whether someone is bisexual will depend on how you ask the question.

Barriers to a Healthy Sexual Identity

Sometimes individuals with a same-sex identity encounter struggles that make it difficult to accept their sexual identity. Online behaviors may be attempts to cope with these struggles. Three related major barriers are homonegativity, heterosexism, and homophobia.

Homonegativity

The biggest example of a barrier is homonegativity. Recent research highlights how internalized negative thoughts about one's self may be the largest contributor to feelings of depression. This depression is often a contributing factor to suicidal thoughts and feelings and increased unsafe sexual behaviors. Might avoiding negative feelings may be associated with your online behavior?

Heterosexism

Another major barrier to a same-sex identity is heterosexism, which is the bias that heterosexuality is superior to all other sexual orientations. Reparative Therapy is one unethical application of heterosexism. Hate crimes are an extreme example of heterosexism, such as the infamous 1998 case of Matthew Shepard, who was attacked, brutally beaten and left to die because he had a same-sex identity. Such attacks hinder individuals' self-discovery process, because a generalized fear leads to withdrawal and increased isolation. Other examples of barriers to a healthy sexual identity include structural barriers such as legal consequences (loss of custody of children), negative stereotypes, internalized shame and family rejection.

Homophobia

Homophobia is another recognized barrier to a healthy lifestyle. It is the irrational fear of homosexuality. This fear leads to avoidance of homosexuality, including the possibility of interacting with healthy role models. What has often been defined as homophobia might actually be better described as heterosexism and homonegativity.

• Review your sexual history. How much of your online behavior was related to components of sexual identity?

• How could you use the Internet to gain additional information about sexual identity?

• What positive, negative or shameful messages have you heard about same-sex and bisexual orientations? How have these affected your sexual health?

Sexual Functioning

What is Sexual Functioning

Sexual health is not merely the avoidance of unhealthy behaviors. It is also the ability and confidence to engage successfully in healthy sexual behaviors. Such ability is defined as Sexual Functioning. For individuals who use the Internet as a coping mechanism for creating sexual arousal, there may be current difficulty to function sexually with their partner. The goal of this section is for you to address your level of sexual functioning, enabling you to examine the relationship between your online sexual behaviors and your sexual functioning, spot issues and develop plans for addressing those issues.

Depending on the cause, there are three potential approaches for treating sexual functioning issues: (1) treating physical health (e.g., getting a physical), (2) treating symptoms (e.g., communication/relaxation) and (3) learning techniques/skills (e.g., performing Kegel exercises, sensation focusing).

A complete medical check-up is the starting point for intervention in cases of sexual dysfunction. If there is a medical condition, no amount of talk therapy will help. (This highlights the importance of being able to talk about sex and sexuality. See, Talking About Sex, page 24.) Your doctor might not raise the issue, so be prepared to mention it yourself. If the medical examination eliminates physical concerns, then the source of the problem might be a mental health concern, such as anxiety or depression (see page 106). Finally, sometimes the intervention may simply be educational. For example, some men do not know how to stimulate the woman's clitoris to help her reach orgasm. That is an example of sexual dysfunction eliminated through discovery and education.

Respond to the following statements:

1. I feel pressured to have sex by my sexual partner(s). [ ] Check here if no current sexual partner. YES / NO

2. I avoid sex because of problems with sexual functioning. YES / NO

3. I do not find sex pleasurable. YES / NO

4. Most of the time, I orgasm "come" too quickly when I am with my partner(s) YES / NO

5. I have concerns about my sexual functioning. YES / NO

6. FOR MEN: I have trouble getting or keeping an erection
FOR WOMEN: I have trouble with lubrication (getting wet). YES / NO

7. I think I might have a sexual functioning problem caused by a medical condition or prescription medications. YES / NO

8. I often have a delay or absence of orgasm when I am with a YES / NO

sexual partner.

9. I have physical pain during sexual intercourse.	YES / NO
10. I usually am able to orgasm or "come" when I am with my partner(s).	YES / NO
11. I think I might have a sexual functioning problem caused by drinking or using illegal drugs.	YES / NO
12. I have no interest in having sex.	YES / NO
13. I am generally satisfied with my sexual behavior.	YES / NO
14. I feel anxious about my ability to perform sexually.	YES / NO
15. I often have a delay or absence of orgasm when I masturbate.	YES / NO
16. I have no interest in having sexual intercourse.	YES / NO
17. FOR MEN: I gave myself a testicular exam in the last 30 days. FOR WOMEN: I gave myself a breast exam in the last 30 days.	YES / NO

Any "yes" response to statements 1–9, 11–12, and 14–16 require further investigation. Any "no" response to statements 10, 13, 16, 17 require further investigation.

The majority of sexual functioning issues include:

General Types of Sexual Dysfunction Issues

The following descriptions of dysfunction are broad and are not intended to address specifics necessary to address particular cases. It is a place for you to start a conversation with your support network.

Problems achieving orgasm

Problems achieving orgasm occur in men and women, yet women experience it more often. Treatment might not be physical and may require medical review. Sometimes, a women's partner needs education to assist her in achieving an orgasm. Side effects of some medications can affect desire and interfere with orgasm. Sexual desire changes over time. Decreased sexual desire is normal in some situations (e.g., as we age). Sometimes, however, it is not normal, such as when caused by medical issues (e.g., hormonal changes or mental health issues). Sexual Aversion is an extreme avoidance or negative reaction to sexuality or sexual behavior. Usually, this is a mental health issue.

Female Physical Dysfunction Issues

Dyspareunia and *Vaginismus* are issues affecting female genitalia. The primary experience is pain in the genital area, usually during penetration. The causes vary, and medical review is required for diagnosis and treatment. Although the majority of causes are medical, psychological issues (such as unresolved abuse issues) can contribute to these conditions.

Male Physical Dysfunction Issues

Male dysfunction issues are categorized as impotence problems and ejaculation problems (premature and retarded). Get a medical check-up to eliminate physical causes, and ask your physician to address any sexual functioning concerns based on biomedical causes or medications. If physical, biomedical and medication-related causes are ruled out, then you should consult a trained therapist. Your particular problem will require a custom tailored intervention. Also, consider what parts of the process in the next section need to be addressed.

Assignment

- Review and update your sexual history and timeline when have you experienced sexual functioning issues? If any, your plans to address these are:

- How have your online behavior contributed to sexual functioning problems?

- Have there been changes in your sexual behavior because of functioning concerns (increased online behaviors, increased masturbation, avoidance of sex, or use of sexually explicit material because of problems with erections or painful penetration)?

- How have your online behaviors been an attempt to cope with sexual functioning?

- Describe any times where you had pain when engaging in sexual behavior? If any, your plans to address these are as follows:

Sexual Functioning and Development of Sexual Skills

People view a typical sexually explicit movie or Internet pornography and they assume – unrealistically - that they need to have sex "like a porn star." The performance expectations created have to be challenged. Real people do not perform sexually the way suggested in pornography. In addition, many individuals struggle with so much sexual shame that they simply shut down any sexual energy. Individuals struggling with sexual anorexia/sexual avoidance may believe they lack the skills needed to engage in sex. For individuals struggling with sexual anxiety, sex evokes such anxiety that it results in unpleasant experiences, creating a cycle leading to additional anxiety. Sexually compulsive individuals sometimes focus on one type of sexual experience at the expense of all other types of sexual intimacy. One goal of sexual health is the development of the knowledge, comfort, and skills for engaging in a variety of forms of sexual expression.

Sexual Health requires self-knowledge, and the awareness to assertively communicate what you want. Some individuals look for a particular type of sexual intimacy, but they don't know how to ask for it. Or – if they do know how to ask for what they are seeking - how to maintain that intimacy. Often, the individual and the partner don't feel comfortable talking about the different types of sexual intimacy. And sometimes, the lack of sexual contact is both a cause – and a result - of online sexual behavior.

As part of the process of addressing sexual functioning issues, clients develop the skills at each level, moving toward increasingly complex skills. In math, you start with addition and subtraction, moving to multiplication and division, then algebra and calculus. Eventually you learn statistics. Our clients first focus on basic skills, later moving toward increasingly complex forms of sexual expression.

Assignment

Following this paragraph is a list of different types of sexual intimacy ranked in increasing levels of intensity In the following assignment, consider how might the Internet negatively or positively influence the sexual intimacies listed below.

Consider each step. (This process can take months). Some steps may be easier than others. It is important to develop and maintain open communication with your partner. Your partner's willingness to participate is crucial; this may require couples therapy. Obviously if you are struggling with intimacy issues, quickies or one-time encounters will interfere with your healing; online behaviors may interfere with the process as well. The key is to move slowly. When you feel anxiety or discomfort, say so, slow down and, if necessary, stop. Comfort at each level is necessary before moving to the next step. After each experience, reflect on and talk about your experience. Doing so will give you insight into what was easy and liked, or difficult and disliked, and ultimately whether you think you are ready to move toward the next step. If something is too uncomfortable or too anxiety producing, you may have to stay at that step for a while, or even return to an earlier step.

Types of Sexual Intimacies

Looking. The place to start is awareness of attraction. What kind of person do you find attractive? What characteristics do you like? Not like? How has the Internet shaped what you find attractive? Has the Internet been helpful? Focus beyond just the physical and include aspects of how the other person talks with you and treats you. What are the other person's values regarding sexuality? Share your responses with your support system. Provide them with examples. Recognizing your attractions leads to the next step.

Flirting. The next step is disclosure to the person to whom you are attracted. Often this is where people get stopped. This step requires addressing fears of rejection. In some cases, rather than dealing with rejection, people either shut down their attractions or settle for someone else. Has the Internet been used to cope with the fear of rejection?

Spending time together. Learning how to spend time together is the next step. Sometimes this may be simply going out to coffee or dinner, or a more formal type of date. Review the discussion on dating (starting on page 167). Dating typically means spending time together. Reflect on how the Internet could be a barrier to spending time together.

Touching. Learning healthy, safe and respectful touch is a next step. This can involve simply holding hands, perhaps dancing or even light kissing. Being able to express what you like and don't like is a part of this process. At this part of the development, the assumption is that you are "clothes on." Future steps will introduce the experience of clothes off. At this point, the goal is to simply be comfortable with touch. How might the Internet negatively or positively influence this step?

Kissing and Petting. At this step, you move toward increased physical touch. It is assumed that the clothes are still on, and that the touch focuses on areas other then genitalia and breasts. You might focus on touching parts of the face, hands, head, etc. As with all other steps, it is important to be aware of what you like/dislike and what feels comfortable/uncomfortable. Ongoing communication with your partner and support system is also assumed. How might the Internet negatively or positively influence this step?

Nurturing and Full Body Touch. In this stage, you still have your clothes on, but the level of touch has increased to the point where multiple parts of the body are touching. You may also be sitting next to each other on a couch, etc., or lying next to each other. This level of touch is sometimes described as "spooning" or laying front to back. As with the previous two steps, starting with touching non-genital parts of the body, moving toward eventual touching the genitals/breasts over the clothes. This part of the process is deeply connected to your image of your body and genitals (see page 129). How might the Internet negatively or positively influence this step?

Nudity. The next level is being next to each other naked. This may have to start slowly, for example, simply being in undergarments before being naked. Again, it is important to start off touching parts of the body other than breasts and genitalia. Once the touch is comfortable, move toward touching your partner's genitalia. Pay attention to thoughts you have as a result of your online sexual behavior.

Masturbation and Mutual Masturbation. Continuing up the scale of intensity, the next step is masturbating yourself in front of your partner and watching your partner masturbate. Many individuals struggle with shame, guilt, and embarrassment around masturbation. Reviewing the discussion on masturbation (see page 133) may be helpful to help you increase self-awareness on this issue. Mutual masturbation (you masturbating your partner and your partner masturbating you) is the next step. At this point, orgasm isn't the goal, simply being comfortable with the level of touch and sexual intimacy is the key. Your level of arousal will ebb and flow, even within the encounter. The goals are being comfortable with your body and being with your partner without expectations. Identify which parts of your body lead to the highest level of arousal and share this information with your partner (i.e., your hot spots!). Perhaps when you are comfortable with the touch, orgasm through masturbation can be introduced at this level. Orgasm may also be introduced at the later stages as well.

Fantasy. Fantasies are extremely powerful. They are far up the scale because they give others a view of the innermost part of the person. It takes a lot of trust to share your fantasy with your partner. Reviewing the discussion on fantasy (see page 137) and discussing your fantasies with your therapist may be helpful before sharing your fantasy with your partner.

Penetration. The next step is developing comfort with sexual intercourse. The first step at this point is feeling comfortable with penetration. Understanding what you like/dislike, and what feels comfortable/uncomfortable is the key. Learning strategies and positions for penetration are required as well. Some people struggle with penetration due to pain, shame, or fear. As with all stages, reflection and conversation with your support system and your partner is important. Notice how views of online sexual behavior shape your assumption of the behavior you're "supposed" to have.

Orgasm. Clinicians disagree whether orgasm is required in the final stage. Many individuals do see it as the goal and they struggle with experiencing an orgasm. Too often, we assume orgasm has to be like the images we see online. And, obviously, orgasm feels great. Orgasm isn't always required or needed. It is included, however, because our goal is to help you develop the skills, comfort, and self-awareness to experience orgasm. At this step, all of what you learned in the previous steps is used to facilitate success at this step. It is difficult to provide universal instructions, so working with your support system and your partner is very important.

Sexual Health Care and Safer-Sex Issues

Respond to the following statements:

1. I feel too embarrassed to buy condoms.   YES / NO

2. I fear getting HIV/AIDS or another sexually transmitted infection.   YES / NO

3. It is my responsibility to use a condom with my sexual partner(s).   YES / NO

4. I would use condoms if my partner asked me.   YES / NO

5. Condoms are embarrassing to use.   YES / NO

6. I want information on feeling better about my sexuality.   YES / NO

7. I have had anal or vaginal sexual intercourse without a condom in the last 30 days.   YES / NO

8. I feel I am at high risk for getting HIV/AIDS or another sexually transmitted infection.	YES / NO
9. I worry I might be infected with a sexually transmitted infection.	YES / NO
10. I want information on sexually transmitted infection.	YES / NO
11. I feel ashamed when seeking medical care for sexually transmitted infections.	YES / NO
12. I feel comfortable when I touch my genitals.	YES / NO
13. Condoms make sex less pleasurable.	YES / NO
14. I have noticed physical genital change in the last 30 days that concern me.	YES / NO
15. My partner would use condoms if I asked him/her.	YES / NO
16. I want information on how to practice safer sex.	YES / NO
17. I worry that I might be infected with HIV. [ ] check here if you know you are HIV+.	YES / NO
18. I want information on HIV/AIDS.	YES / NO
19. I know how to use a condom correctly.	YES / NO
20. I engaged in unsafe sexual behavior in the last 30 days.	YES / NO

Score 1 point for each "yes" response to the following statements: 1–2, 5–7, 8–11, 13–14, 16–18, 20. Score 1 point for each "no" response to the following statements: 3, 4, 12, 15, 19. The higher the score, the increased risk to your overall sexual health and HIV/STI.

The questions above reflect research into the relationship between sexual health and safer-sex concerns that underlie increased risk for HIV transmission and sexually transmitted infection (STIs). They also reflect areas of focus in your progress toward improved sexual health. The purpose of this topic is to review HIV and STIs as they relate to your sexual behavior. This topic does not focus on prevention, (see http://www.cdc.gov/hiv/default.htm) or treatment issues (see http://www.thebody.com/). Together, the two websites cover a range of topics, from prevention techniques, resources and responses to commonly asked questions about HIV/AIDS and STIs. Although prevention and treatment issues are important, the goal of this topic is to help you understand how sexual health relates to your sexual behavior. To maintain and create sexual health, it is important to understand the thoughts you have about HIV, STIs and sexual behavior.

In the field of HIV/STI prevention, there is significant research into why people engage in unsafe sexual behavior. The research has generally suggested a number of themes relevant to sexual health including sexual compulsivity, mood, alcohol and drug use, and sexual functioning concerns. Reflect on the times you have engaged in unsafe behaviors. Which reasons appear to be more relevant for you? Include these issues in your continuing care plan.

In this approach, unsafe sexual behaviors are not the problem, but a symptom of something more. The relationship between sexual health and safer-sex behaviors can be multidirectional. For example, your mood can shape your sexual behavior, and your reaction to that behavior may set you up for the next round of your cycle. You might think, "I'm so ashamed of my behavior that my feelings of hopelessness and worthlessness have increased." The helpful part of this reality is that intervening in the process at any point is a start toward improving sexual health.

Working with clients whose self-hatred, shame, guilt, depression and/or hopelessness contribute to their unsafe sexual behaviors has been one of our saddest experiences. We've heard too many times "I wanted to kill myself by getting HIV." This is a classic example of why sexual health has so many components, and it highlights the difficulty many people have in moving toward sexual health. In these situations, sexual health requires addressing the underlying issues. Much of that material applies to safer-sex issues: "If I believe I'm worthless, and I can get affirmation through sex, I will do whatever my sexual partner wants in order to get them to stay with me, including breaking my personal guidelines for safer-sex."

While a depressed mood can contribute to high-risk behaviors, anxiety around HIV can cause some people to simply shut down their sexual expression. The anxiety leads to paralysis and fear. In some cases, the anxiety leads to sexual health concerns through ritual masturbation, sexual avoidance or use of sexually explicit material. The high level of anxiety in response to HIV can lead some people to use alcohol and drugs as a way to self-medicate and reduce the level of their anxiety. While under the influence, they might engage in unsafe sexual behavior that creates feelings of shame and guilt.

Bringing these three themes together (high risk behaviors as symptoms, depression and anxiety), it is easy to see how online behaviors may be related to sexual health and HIV. Out of fear of HIV, clients will reduce their behavior to only online behaviors thinking, "Online virtual sex is safer sex. I don't have to worry about getting infected." On the other end of the continuum, online behaviors can lead to increased unsafe sexual behavior. People will chat online before they hook up. While chatting, they'll ask, are you positive/negative? (Do you have HIV? Positive is slang for "yes," and negative is slang for "no.") Sometimes, people believe the other person's answer and engage in higher risk behaviors as a result.

Assignment

- The last time I talked with my doctor about HIV/STIs was? The last time I was screened for HIV/STIs was? My plans to speak with the doctor are:

- Describe the connection between your online behaviors and safer sex concerns. How do you behaviors change in light of HIV and Sexually Transmitted Illnesses?

- Review your unsafe sexual behavior. Highlight at least 4–5 reasons for unsafe sexual behavior that are relevant to you.

- My personal safer-sex plans to address my unsafe sexual behavior are:

Barriers to Sexual Health

Over the next few pages we review the major barriers to sexual health, including mental health issues and abuse. We briefly highlight additional barriers that may be present. As you discover your own personal barriers, please consult with a trained professional if these are significant issues in your life.

Mental Health Factors

One of the largest barriers to sexual health is the presence of mental health factors. We will highlight four major mental health concerns most frequently associated with Internet sexual compulsivity: Attention Deficit Hyperactivity Disorder, Depression, Bi-Polar Disorder and Anxiety Disorders. The overlap between mood disorders and sexual health concerns is so common that the question is not, "Is there a mood disorder present?" but "*Which* mood disorder is present?" As with other areas discussed in the book, the connection between online behaviors and mental health concerns is probably bi-directional: people use the Internet to cope with a mental health concern; and the Internet behavior contributes to increased mental health problems.

Mood disorder is the term used to describe a person's difficulty understanding, coping with, and managing a variety of feelings. Sometimes, people's feelings are out of control and they simply don't know what to do. Sexual behavior can be an attempt to cope with the feelings or, vice-versa, the sexual behavior may trigger a series of feelings that appear out of control.

Understandably, some people initially avoid a diagnosis of a mood disorder, because the language and cultural response often are negative and judgmental. Please be open to the possibility that you are suffering from a mood disorder. Acknowledging a mood disorder actually creates hope, because we have language to understand and strategies to treat the symptoms.

ADHD and the Internet

Studies have reported an association between Internet compulsivity and attention deficit/hyperactivity disorder (ADHD). Most often, ADHD is first recognized in childhood or adolescence. Recently, adults are being diagnosed with ADHD more frequently. The diagnosis of adult ADHD is controversial, because the diagnosis of ADHD in adults is viewed by some as a "trendy" diagnosis rather than a true problem. Also, a diagnosis of adult ADHD is open to misuse, particularly when it provides an excuse for the behavior. E.g., "I go online because I have ADHD."

Undoubtedly, there is a relationship between Internet use and ADHD, but the research does not demonstrate whether one causes the other. (Understanding relational research can be challenging. In one example, ice cream sales and crime rates are related: both increase and decrease at the same time. But that does not mean that one causes the other. So, even though it is tempting to conclude, "People steal money to buy ice cream," or, "Eating ice cream leads to crime," neither is accurate. Actually, both ice cream sales and crime rates increase in warm weather, because more people are outside in warm weather (and hence may be robbed), and also because more people eat ice cream during warm weather.)

The key in our work involving ADHD is to acknowledge the relationship between ADHD and the Internet, and provide a basic level of information for you to follow-up with your primary physician. In some cases, treating ADHD might reduce an individual's problems with the Internet. To help you determine if you need follow-up, please review the following symptoms. If five or six of them describe you, please seek out and obtain the necessary support.

Symptoms of ADHD include:

- Does not give close attention to details.
- Makes careless mistakes in work, or other activities.
- Often has trouble keeping attention on tasks.

- Often does not seem to listen when spoken to directly.
- Often does not follow through on instructions.
- Fails to finish duties in the workplace.
- Often has trouble organizing activities.
- Doesn't want to do things that take a lot of mental effort.
- Often loses things.
- Is often easily distracted.
- Is often forgetful in daily activities.
- Often fidgets with hands or feet or squirms in seat when sitting still is expected.
- Often gets up from seat when remaining in seat is expected.
- Often feel very restless.
- Often has trouble doing leisure activities quietly.
- Is often "on the go" or often acts as if "driven by a motor".
- Often talks excessively.
- Often blurts out answers before questions have been finished.
- Often has trouble waiting one's turn.
- Often interrupts or intrudes on others (e.g., butts into conversations or games).

Depression

Without a doubt, a major issue related to sexual health is depression. In non-technical terms, statements such as "I'm sad" or "I don't have any energy" might be expressions of depression. Other behavioral indicators might be not eating or not getting out of bed. It is easy to see how online sexual behavior can occur in response to feeling depressed, either through going online for sexual behavior to feel good, or shutting down sexually. Sometimes the shame of online behavior may reflect a bigger issue of depression. The goal here is to review depression in such a way that you might recognize how depression and online sexual health concerns are related.

One difficulty in recognizing the presence of depression is that sometimes depression may be part of a bigger issue. For example, the next issues we will cover are bipolar disorder, manic episodes and post-traumatic stress disorders. In each of these issues, depression may be a symptom of the other conditions. It may take some time for an accurate assessment that describes all of your symptoms. We've listed a number of symptoms below that are ranked according to seriousness of the symptoms. If three or more of these symptoms are present, we strongly recommend you seek additional help.

> **If you are experiencing suicidal thoughts, or feelings**, get immediate help at http://www.helpguide.org/mental/suicide_help.htm, call **1-800-273-TALK**, call **911** or visit your **local emergency room**. Suicidal thoughts are the most severe symptoms. Clinicians are trained to respond respectfully and immediately.

Symptoms of Depression (In descending order of severity)

- A suicide attempt.
- A specific plan for committing suicide.
- Recurrent suicidal ideation ("I want to die") without a specific plan.
- Recurrent thoughts of death (not just fear of dying).
- Depressed mood most of the day, nearly every day.
- People reporting to you that you look depressed.
- Feelings of irritability.
- Fatigue or loss of energy nearly every day.
- Feelings of worthlessness or excessive/inappropriate guilt.
- Loss of pleasure or interest in daily activities.
- Significant weight loss when not dieting (e.g., a change of more than 5% of body weight in a month).
- Decrease or increase in appetite nearly every day.
- Sleeping too much (can't get out of bed).
- Sleeping too little (can't fall asleep).
- Feelings of agitation; body is restless.
- No energy; body feels weary.
- Difficulty making decisions.
- Difficulty thinking or concentrating.

There are some issues that disqualify a mental-health diagnosis. Sometimes a more important/severe diagnosis takes priority. Or, if you've taken drugs or chemicals (e.g., alcohol) you might have a different diagnosis. In some cases, a medical condition might be a cause of some of the symptoms. Again, the key is to seek the advice of a professional if three or more of the above symptoms are present.

Bipolar Disorder/Manic-Depression

Another mood disorder related to sexual health concerns is bipolar disorder. (The disorder is sometimes labeled "manic-depression.") As with anxiety and depression, bipolar disorder exists on a continuum of severity. Very few people experience the extreme form of the symptoms, officially labeled as "Bipolar I." Severe forms of bipolar disorder are difficult to manage and require a multidisciplinary approach, including psychiatrists, therapists and a strong support network. The other forms of bipolar disorder are less-severe expressions and are probably more frequent and less recognized. Because they are less recognized, it is important to examine the descriptions and symptoms to see if one of the less-severe expressions might be present in relation to your sexual behavior. If symptoms are present, please check with a mental-health professional for further assessment and treatment.

Listed below are some symptoms of manic episodes. If you experience three or more of these symptoms, please consult with a mental-health professional. If all the symptoms occur during the same time window (say, within a week), the "episode" may be labeled "manic." If the number of symptoms is fewer or the duration of the symptoms is shorter, the episode may be labeled "hypomanic." The intensity and number of symptoms often reflect the severity of the diagnosis.

Symptoms of manic episodes

- Increased energy, activity and restlessness.
- Excessively "high" euphoric mood.
- Extreme irritability.
- Racing thoughts and talking very fast.
- Jumping from one idea to another.
- Distractibility; can't concentrate well.
- Little sleep needed.
- Unrealistic beliefs in one's abilities and powers.
- Excessive self-esteem or grandiosity.
- Spending sprees.
- Increased sexual drive.
- Abuse of drugs, particularly methamphetamine, cocaine, alcohol and sleeping medications.
- Provocative, intrusive or aggressive behavior.

- Denial that anything is wrong.
- Overbearing behaviors that cross other people's boundaries.
- Dramatic increase in social or work-oriented activities.

Bipolar disorder usually reflects a swing from a manic to a depressive mood. Review the section on symptoms of depression. If you experience symptoms of both depression and bipolar disorder, a different treatment approach may be necessary. What makes bipolar disorder hard to assess is the difficulty recognizing a less-than-full-blown depressive episode or a less-than-full-blown manic episode. Clients will often recognize signs of depression and obtain treatment for that condition, but are so grateful for the relief from the depression when in a manic or hypomanic stage that they don't see themselves as having further problems, such as bipolar disorder. Because of the emotional exhaustion of being in the depression stage, simply having energy is such a welcome relief for individuals with depression, that they do not seek further treatment.

Anxiety

Another important mood disorder to consider is anxiety and whether it has a role in your sexual behavior. Think about how anxiety is present and shapes your online behavior, or use of the Internet to avoid other sexual behavior. Anxiety, in the simplest sense, is a sense of fear or uneasiness. Some anxiety is helpful in that it motivates us. For instance, you might say, "I'm nervous that my boss will get upset if I don't complete the project by Friday, so I'm going to commit to completing it." In these cases, anxiety is a positive thing. In some situations, however, anxiety can be a serious problem for people. In extreme cases, anxiety disorders can be debilitating.

If anxiety becomes pronounced, it can express itself in various ways. For example, you may have trouble sleeping. You might find you dwell on a particular situation and find it difficult to concentrate on other things. Your appetite or eating behaviors might change. Alternatively, you might have a sense of vigilance or a feeling of impending disaster, as if "something bad is going to happen." In some cases, anxiety can mask other mental-health issues such as depression. Below are symptoms and types of anxiety. Ask yourself, "How do these symptoms show up in my life?" If you experience two or three symptoms, please seek professional help for additional consultation.

Symptoms/types of anxiety

- Feelings of apprehension or dread.
- Trouble concentrating.
- Feeling tense and jumpy.
- Anticipating the worst.
- Irritability.
- Restlessness.
- Watching for signs of danger.
- Feeling like your mind's gone blank.
- Pounding heart.
- Sweating.
- Stomach upset or dizziness.
- Frequent urination or diarrhea.
- Shortness of breath.
- Tremors and twitches.
- Muscle tension.
- Headaches.
- Fatigue.
- Insomnia.

Treatment for Mental Health Issues

Treatments for mental health issues vary. We encourage you to go online and search for strategies addressing the mental health issue relevant in your life. If you are working with a counselor, please ask about your counselor's level of expertise and comfort with a particular type of therapy. If you want to try something on the list below and your primary counselor can't provide the resources, it is your right to ask for a referral to a therapist who can. Here are a just a few possible treatment approaches:

Medication Management

The number and type of medications are constantly changing, so please consult with a trained professional. Many individuals are not interested in this treatment approach because of fear and stigma regarding medications, but at times the use of medication is appropriate. For example, let's say you've broken your foot. For a while, you'll need crutches for support as your foot heals. Think of medication as a similar support that can help you while you address the issues related to mood disorder. Also look at the example of diabetes treatment. Some people manage their diabetes through diet and exercise, and do not require medication. For some, however, long-term insulin use is required to stay healthy. Similarly, long-term use of medications may be needed for mental health. You and your doctor can work on the best fit and plan.

Talk Therapy

Talk therapy takes a range of approaches. The number and type of interventions are simply too many to list, but some of the better known therapies include:

- Cognitive-Behavioral Therapy (CBT).
- Dialectical Behavioral Therapy (DBT) Skills.
- Supportive Talk Therapy.
- Eye Movement Desensitization and Reprocessing (EMDR) Therapy.
- Relationship Therapy.

Alternative Therapies

- Recreational Therapy Activities such as Challenge Courses
- Eastern approaches such as Acupuncture, Yoga, and Massage.

Healthy Daily Activities[11]

One way to cope with mood disorders is to develop healthy habits that help balance the mood and help you create stability and balance in your life. Here are a few examples:

- Talk with someone. Ask trusted friends and acquaintances to spend time with you daily, preferably face to face.
- Wait until you are feeling better before attempting difficult tasks.
- Make a written schedule for yourself every day and stick to it.
- Get at least eight hours of sleep each night.
- Get out into the sun or into nature for at least 30 minutes a day.
- Make time for things that bring you joy.

Manage Your Diet

Managing your diet is another way to help with stabilizing your mood.

- Stop or reduce your consumption of products that contain caffeine, such as coffee, tea, cola and chocolate.
- Stop or reduce your consumption of products that contain nicotine (a stimulant).
- Review over-the-counter medicines or herbal remedies. Many contain chemicals that can affect mood.

Exercise/Relaxation

A holistic approach to treating mood disorders can facilitate balance, including:

- Exercise daily.
- Muscle tension is commonly experienced in the back of the neck and shoulders. One easy way to get rid of such tension is to tighten the neck and shoulders, holding for 5–10 seconds before releasing.
- Close your eyes, take a deep breath through the nose, exhale through your mouth and repeat a few times. When breathing in, let your stomach expand as much as possible. Concentrate on breathing slowly and calmly, thinking of your slow breathing as calming your entire body.

Meditation Activities

The following activities can help you focus your thoughts, as well as express feelings regarding factors associated with the mood disorder.

- Draw.
- Write in a Journal.
- Listen to relaxing music.
- Tell yourself "I am relaxed" as you carry out breathing exercises.
- Visualize a soothing image (e.g. lying on a warm beach).

Assignment

- In the sexual behavioral timeline (see page 36), you chart your life along the horizontal axis. The +5 to 0 range is to help you start thinking about your moods. Look at the symptoms of anxiety, depression and bipolar disorder. Which symptoms are present? Update your timeline by graphing these symptoms across your lifetime.

- Could a mood disorder impair your sexual functioning?

- Might online sexual behavior be attempts to reduce symptoms of the mood disorder?

- Might your online sexual behaviors be a contributing factor to a mood disorder?

- Identify your plans to address any concerns raised in this topic.

Types and Impact of Abuse

It is important to review the relationship between abuse/neglect and your sexual timeline and online sexual behavior. The topic of types and degrees of abuse and neglect is too complex for a complete discussion here, but the following is a brief review. Treatment approaches vary and are not reviewed here. Please seek professional help if abuse or neglect is part of your history.

The major types of abuse – physical, emotional, sexual – are categorized to help describe the abuse, but types of abuse may overlap.

Physical Abuse

Physical abuse includes any behavior that causes or contributes to a physical injury to another person. The abuse can be direct or indirect. Direct abuse is when the perpetrator causes the physical contact. Indirect abuse is when a third object is involved. For example, if your neighbor hits you with her fist, she made *direct* contact with you. If she threw a lamp at you and missed, but to get out of the way you tripped, fell and bruised yourself, then she was an *indirect* cause of the injury. However, since she threw the lamp in the first place, she is ultimately a cause of the abuse.

Examples of physical abuse include the following:

- Getting hit.
- Getting hit with an object.
- Hair pulling.
- Being burned.
- Being cut.
- Someone stopping you from breathing for a short period of time.
- Administering a harmful substance or any substance that results in harm.
- Physical injury.

Sexual Abuse

Sexual abuse can include a range of behaviors. These include extreme forms of abuse such as rape, molestation, forced prostitution or incest. Other forms of sexual abuse include exploitation, use of a power relationship (teacher/student, caretaker/child, therapist/client). Less extreme forms of abuse can include manipulation of others for sexual pleasure, voyeurism and exhibitionism. Sexual abuse also includes sexual harassment and verbal degradation. Sexual contact by an adult with a person under the legal age of consent is by statute a form of sexual assault and results in automatic criminal charges if revealed. Other examples of sexual abuse include the following:

- Sexual innuendoes or provocative statements.
- Engaging in sexual behavior in front of another person.
- Exposing one's genitals to another person without permission.
- Fondling or touching another's breast or genital area.

- An adult or older child engaging a child in sexual intercourse, masturbation, oral sex, or genital sex.
- Adult sexual contact, such as sexual intercourse, masturbation or oral-genital sex without permission or when permission is withdrawn.

Emotional Abuse

The third classic type of abuse is emotional abuse. This involves negative statements being directed toward you. Some incidents of emotional abuse might be one-time events, but often there is a pervasive pattern of negative statements.

Examples of emotional abuse include the following:

- Name-calling.
- Put-downs.
- Failure to affirm.
- Shaming.
- Judgmentalism.
- Making threats.
- Yelling.

Overt and Covert Abuse

A lot of research and practice emphasizes addressing overt abuse, which is "abuse that is easily recognized." If you review the previous examples, it's easy to recognize whether something did or did not happen. There usually is a specific person, behavior, event, time and place when a person describes the abuse. In therapy, a client will say, "My partner did. . . ." and then describe in great detail what happened.

Covert abuse is equally as damaging but is often hidden or covered and not recognized. We apply the label of covert abuse to any setting where there is an atmosphere of fear. Therefore, statements such "I can give you something to cry about" creates an atmosphere of impending physical abuse. Another example: "Don't make me get the belt." A third example is "Wait until your father gets home." These behaviors are covert physical abuse. The difficulty, however is that covert abuse is difficult to recognize. A client may sense something is wrong, but not have awareness of a specific problem. A client may report being vigilant for no apparent reason. But the threat of abuse causes such a client to shudder simply because of a look from a partner, friend, or parent. The threat or feelings of fear are the keys to recognizing covert abuse. Review each type of abuse. How might covert abuse be present in your life?

Abuse and Neglect

Abuse is typically an active behavior. (I "did" something, or something was "done" to me). Just as damaging is neglect. Neglect is the failure to provide the necessary resources to another person. Emotional and physical neglect is often recognizable. Emotional neglect can be the failure to provide emotional support. Physical neglect can be the failure to provide appropriate nutrition, shelter or clothing. Sexual neglect could be the failure to provide adequate sexual education. Both covert abuse and neglect are very difficult to recognize. It is only after the fact and through the review of the indicators of abuse that a person can identify covert abuse and/or neglect.

Sexual Violence

Sexual violence is any type of sexual activity that you do not agree to. The amount of sexual violence in our society remains at epidemic proportions. Instances of sexual violence are notoriously underreported. Some scholars have suggested 3% of college women experience sexual assault in a given year.[12] Another article suggests 25% of girls and 16% of boys are abused before age 16.[13] Furthermore, professionals rarely recognize the concept of male-on-male rape as an issue and often do not provide treatment for victims.[14] Examples of sexual violence (usually referred to as sexual assault and abuse) include the following:

- Inappropriate touching (such as the grabbing of your breasts, butt or penis, or brushing up against you without your consent), whether it is intentional or *ostensibly* by accident.
- Vaginal, anal or oral penetration, or attempted penetration (with or without objects), without your consent.
- Being spied on (i.e., voyeurism).
- Having someone expose himself or herself to you without your consent.
- Sexual contact when consent is not present. (The concept of consent is covered in the topic Sexual Behavior and Expression on page 154.)

Sexual violence can occur to anyone at any time. A relative or person known to the victim is the most common perpetrator of this kind of violence. When a partner, wife, husband or dating partner is the perpetrator, the abuse is defined as "domestic rape" or "date rape." The rise of date rape drugs exacerbates the problem and provides a barrier to seeking help. While sensationalized in the movies, stranger rape is less common, though it still occurs and is important to assess. If you are a victim of sexual violence, seek immediate help. Sometimes an individual does not seek immediate help for any number of reasons. It is never too late to seek help. This can include talking to a therapist, friend or religious advisor. The key is to remember that you are not alone, and that recovering from this experience is possible.

Indicators of Abuse

Below are typical symptoms that abused or neglected individuals experience. They are not always associated with abuse, but these are the early warning signs professionals look for. Review the indicators and compare them with your sexual history. If present, seek additional support.

Physical Indicators of Abuse

- Displays agitation or anger, uncontrollable behaviors, tantrums.
- Displays anxious behaviors (nail biting, teeth grinding, rocking, etc.).
- Often belittles self ("I'm bad, evil, etc.").
- Resists authority or desperately tries to please because they fear repercussions.
- Exhibits excessive guilt.
- Shows fear of a particular person or place.
- Thoughts involve themes of sexual acts, torture, bondage, humiliation and/or abuse.
- Hurts others sexually or physically.
- Acts aggressively around pets.
- A child mimicking adult sexual behavior (such as intercourse, French kissing, etc.)
- A child having age-inappropriate sexual knowledge.
- Increased chemical use.
- Increased sexual behavior.

Emotional Indicators of Abuse

- Individual has lots of new fears.
- Shows inappropriate emotions or no emotions at all.

- Fearful others hate them, are angry, want to hurt them, punish them or kill them.
- Fearful someone is "after them" or going to hurt them; wary of strangers.
- Has low self-esteem.
- Is unable to form friendships.
- Is self-destructive; intentionally inflicts harm on self.
- Appears to be "in a fog."
- Has excessive mood swings.
- Suicidal thoughts, statements or gestures

Personal Victimization History

The consequences of abuse vary, and can contribute to relationship, sexual and other problems. Sometimes a person's abuse history contributes to problematic sexual behaviors and chemical use. A common theme in sexual avoidance is a history of abuse. Due to an experience of abuse, a person may have difficulty recognizing and expressing feelings and empathizing with others. Often, people may not label the events as abuse because they don't recognize that they aren't at fault. They say they liked or respected the perpetrator or they could not believe the person would harm them. Sometimes a person thinks the abuse is a normal part of life. Victims have sometimes reported feelings of confusion because they liked the attention or they physically responded to the sexual touch.

Review the above indicators of abuse. Consider if any indicators are present. Might there be a particular event or source of the indicators? To recover from abuse, work with a therapist trained to address these issues.

Assignment

- One assignment we suggest once the client is stable (i.e., not experiencing suicidal thoughts or showing major symptoms of post-traumatic stress disorder) is to work on an abuse history. Include the details such as your age, who, what, when, where and your reaction at the time. Update your timeline as appropriate. Also include your reaction today. Reflect on how the abuse affected you, and identify how it has influenced both your real time and online sexual behavior. In writing your abuse history, include:

  - Physical, sexual, emotional abuse.
  - Overt and covert abuse.

- Experiences with both abuse and neglect.
- Experiences of sexual violence

- Have you experienced sexual violence? What changes in your life occurred as a result? What help have you received? What help would you have liked to receive? What help do you need?

- How is your online sexual behavior related to abuse?

- What are your plans to help you heal and grow?

Recovery from Abuse

If you are in immediate danger, you need a safe place. There are treatment programs, and/or shelters available. Look for Domestic Abuse or Sexual Violence programs in your local area. We encourage you to find help. Our experience is that this can be a significant process for many clients.

Once stable, tell your story. And then tell your story again and again. Group support/therapy is helpful. The decrease in shame, fear and isolation that occurs through group therapy can be powerful. Understanding that "I'm not alone" and "Someone understands" is a powerful source of hope. We often have clients complete an "abuse history" describing the life history of abuse. For some people this is too difficult. We acknowledge healing is a long process. Sharing your story once is only the start. If you need to start slow, simply listing events is the place to start. We adapt the assignment to be: "Describe 4 (or whatever number) events of abuse in your life." Sometimes, simply acknowledging, "I've been abused" is the first step.

Once you know your history, understand the things that trigger flashbacks and struggles in your current daily functioning. You'll need to develop plans to address the triggers. As you move forward, ask yourself what you want your life to look like. This is the hardest place to get to in therapy. The level of fear and lack of hope will need to be resolved prior to this place.

Journaling has two benefits. It is part of the therapy process, but it also helps to remind you of your progress. When you are frustrated, it is helpful to look back and recognize where you've been, what you've come through, and where you're going. Some clients "beat themselves up" because they can't talk to everyone at a party because they are uncomfortable. A journal can highlight the amazing progress signified by simply getting to an event. Journaling doesn't have to mean writing. With new technologies, journaling can include video recordings, art or other forms of expression.

Other possible barriers to sexual health

What follows are two issues that we think are important based on clinical experience. We included them here to focus on the barriers these issues create.

Feelings of Grief

Grief is an issue sometimes connected with sexual health concerns and in particular relationship history. Various theories have explained the process of grief. We like best the model presented by Elizabeth Kübler-Ross, who identified five stages of grief: denial, anger, bargaining, depression and acceptance.

As others have also done, we've made a few tweaks to Kübler-Ross's model to include the role of perceived losses, the role of small losses and the "time focus" of grief. Feelings of grief typically result from a significant loss, such as a death of a loved one, but grief from other losses can also have a powerful impact on a person's life. Take, for instance, the end of a relationship or friendship, or the loss of a job. Grief may also be due to the loss of hopes, dreams or fantasies. For example, in a gay person's coming-out process, the person may feel a loss, because recognizing a same-sex identity ends the perception of a "normal" life. Sometimes, the symbolic meaning of an event, location or person triggers an experience of loss. Moving from your home results in recognition of the end of a sense of security. These perceived losses could have the same impact as a tangible loss.

Some feelings of grief are anticipatory; in this situation, you might foresee the end of something. This may show up as "This is a bad relationship; I need to get out of it, so I go online, I can avoid having to deal with the bad relationship."

One of the critiques of Kübler-Ross's model is the perception that the process of coping with grief is linear; you simply go from one stage to the next. We think grief is cyclical; you might see the parts of a stage a number of times. You may move from acceptance back to denial, etc. We believe the key is to recognize that, whatever the situation, it is acceptable and healthy to be present when experiencing your thoughts and feelings.

A second critique of the Kübler-Ross model is the implication that process occurs once and is rather quick. It is important to remember that coping with a loss takes awhile. In some circumstances, the grief process can last a year or more. In addition, you can trigger grief when certain rituals, anniversaries or memories occur. Our culture often minimizes the long-term impact of grief.

As you review your sexual history, pay attention to how the following stages of grief may have played out. A few examples describe how people might experience the stage.

Stages of Grief

Denial

The goal in this stage is to avoid dealing with the intensity of the grief. This can include actively avoiding the grief or minimizing the loss. Behaviors in this stage include not talking about the loss, glossing over it, or providing a minimal response to avoid further discussion such as "I'm fine" or "It's no big deal."

Anger

In this stage, the energy around coping with grief goes outward. The person may feel victimized or attacked. "This isn't fair." Statements regarding men might include "All men are like that."

Bargaining

In this stage, there is recognition of grief, but the coping mechanism leads one to minimize the impact of grief. A person might begin dating before the grief is resolved (a rebound relationship). Another way this may be present is selecting a new partner with the thought that "He or she is better than no one" or "He or she isn't like the last one." Or, still, "I'll just go online so I don't get hurt."

Depression

Common thoughts in this stage include "Why try?" "Nothing matters" or even "It will never get better." One of the difficulties in distinguishing between depression and grief is that depression is part of the grief process. Review the discussion of depression (see page 108). Might any of the depression symptoms you're experiencing be related to grief?

Acceptance

By this point, the person integrates grief into the person's life, and while grief may be present, it has lost most of its intensity. This means you can acknowledge the loss, but the loss does not result in a barrier to healthy relationships or daily functioning. In some cases, the loss may actually facilitate transformation. These are signs of successful adjustment to grief.

Assignment

Part 1:

Take a piece of paper and create five columns. In the first column, list 75-100 experiences of real, perceived, major and/or minor experiences of loss. You might think that 100 experiences is a lot, but people can identify more losses than they realize. This part of the assignment can take days or weeks to complete. Complete this part of the assignment before you move on to the other columns.

In the second column, explain why this loss still holds so much power now. In the third column, identify possible thinking errors associated with the loss. The fourth column examines the relationship to your online behavior and the final column is to help you start moving forward with a plan. The examples below can be helpful.

Example of Grief Analysis

Type of Loss	Explanation	Related to online behaviors	Plans and Corrections	Connection to sexual health
Major loss (death) Minor loss (plans cancelled) Real loss (relationship ended) Perceived loss (loss of my idea how the future should look).	How does it impact me today? Why does this loss hold so much power?	How is this experience of grief related to my online behaviors? I won't get hurt	How will I address this loss? Is the loss based on a thinking error? If so, what is my correction?	How is this a sexual health issue? What are my plans? I want intimacy
Example 1: My partner left me.	I feel alone and hurt. I feel shame I will never find anyone. Nobody loves me.	My partner had an affair online	I will talk about it with my support group and therapist. I will read a book on dating.	I'm lonely. It's my fault
Example 2: I did not get the job.	I'm no good. They do not like me.	Online behavior fills the time and decreases feelings of boredom	I can find another job. My job does not define me.	I'm worthless. (Thinking error)
Example 3: I am gay.	I will not be able to have children. Everybody judges me. I will be alone. It is a sin.	No one can find out; I'll go online. Only place I can meet people is online.	I could adopt. There are happy gay people in connected, loving relationships. Not everyone believes it is a sin; in fact, some people think it is a blessing.	Gay folks can't be in a relationship (thinking error)

Part 2:

• Describe circumstances when you've felt feelings of grief. How has this related to your online sexual behavior (is the grief a consequence of the behavior, or is grief a cause of the online behavior)?

- When you find yourself feeling grief, what other feelings may be associated with the grief?

- What are your plans to improve your ability to express grief in healthy ways?

Feelings of Anger

Anger is a difficult topic to address because of its web-like relationship to many topics. It is robust, with multiple meanings and ways of being expressed. We summarize a number of issues regarding anger as they may relate to sexual health. If these are relevant, please work with your network to obtain support and additional resources. What makes anger so difficult to understand and treat is the confusion around the phrase "I'm angry."

Sometimes, anger is a primary feeling. Feelings of anger, rage, frustration and disappointment reflect different intensities of anger. The things that trigger the feelings of anger vary. Sometimes anger is a secondary feeling – a response to other feelings. The concept of "flight or fight" demonstrates the difficulty of analyzing anger. When people experience fear, they typically want either to run away or attack the source of the fear. In these cases, anger is actually a response to fear. Treatment should focus on the source of fear. Anger may be a response to being hurt. For some people, their sexual behavior is a form of revenge to hurt another person. Anger can be a part of a process. In the discussion of Feelings of Grief (see page 122), the stages of grief show how anger is a normal part of the grieving process. These three examples demonstrate the importance of understanding why you feel angry. If your feelings of anger are in response to another feeling, it is important to identify and address the primary feeling instead of the anger.

In circumstances where you experience loss, it is helpful to understand how anger is part of the process of healing. One book that might be helpful is *Anger Management for Dummies,* or any other book that you find helpful.

Strategies for Coping with Anger

Mindfulness

In the topic on the Power of Thought (see page 46), we discussed the technique of becoming aware of your body, thoughts and feelings. This skill is also helpful in coping with and expressing anger.

Timeouts

Give yourself a brief break from the situation can reduce unhealthy expressions of anger. We encourage clients to tell themselves, "I need 15 minutes to settle down and think about what I need to say."

Assertive Communication

Review the upcoming discussion on Assertive Communication (see page 145). It is important to learn how to communicate assertively when you feel anger.

Relaxation

Reducing overall stress and identifying ways to relax creates opportunities to focus on what is important and how you want to respond.

Meditation/Journaling

The ability to reflect on an encounter where you felt anger can improve your ability to understand the source of your reaction. Assessing your behavior can improve future responses.

Reaching out

Reaching out to your support network for support, coaching, feedback and advice when you feel anger is also helpful. A different perspective sometimes is needed.

Anger as an Issue for Follow-up

Every once in a while we have a client who has significant problems expressing, managing and coping with feelings of anger. They may use the Internet as an attempt to cope with the anger, or a way to avoid anger. Sometimes the Internet is the center of the problem creating anger (relationship conflict) that only leads to increased online behavior.

As you look at the possibility of improving your coping skills with anger, it is important to focus on healthy anger expression. In some circumstances, clients are abusive toward others. Most often, the abuse is verbal, but in some situations the client will engage in physical abuse. It is *never* acceptable to express anger in this way. In a similar way, attempts to avoid any and all anger are signs of a problem. If you find that you are struggling to cope with the anger, or your anger continues to escalate after using the strategies above, then additional support is recommended, including anger management classes or therapy.

Assignment

- Describe circumstances when you've felt anger.

- How is anger related to your online sexual behavior (e.g., is the anger a consequence of the behavior, or is anger a cause of the online behavior)?

- When you find yourself angry, what other feelings may be associated with the anger?

- What are your plans to improve your ability to express anger in healthy ways?

Body Image

Another component of sexual health is body image. Sexual health involves challenging the stereotypical and cultural images of beauty and encouraging self-acceptance. In order to do this you have to develop a realistic and positive body image. The necessary work in moving toward sexual health suggests this is a major issue for many people. Body image is the foundation for so many parts of our perceptions, internal messages, external messages and feelings that its impact is difficult to address.

Respond to the following statements:

1. In general, I like how my body looks.   YES / NO

2. I like the look of my genitals.   YES / NO

3. I feel I am too thin.   YES / NO

4. I like how my breasts/chest looks.   YES / NO

5. I am uncomfortable with several parts of my body.   YES / NO

6. It is important for me to make my body look good.   YES / NO

7. I have had cosmetic surgery to change my looks.   YES / NO

8. Overall, I feel my body is attractive.   YES / NO

9. FOR MEN: I like the size of my penis.

   FOR WOMEN: I like the size of my breasts.   YES / NO

10. I want to look more masculine.   YES / NO

11. I want to look more feminine.   YES / NO

Score 1 point for each "no" answer to statements 1–4 and 6–9. Score 1 point for each "yes" answer to statements 5, 10–11. The higher the score, the bigger is the concern with body image issues.

What is considered beautiful changes culturally across time. The key to addressing body image is to acknowledge the role of culture (see page 77) and that beauty is based entirely on thought (review the Power of Thought on page 43). Clients who struggle with online sexual compulsivity will often place unrealistic expectations on themselves and their partners. Without a doubt, mainstream American culture worships the perfect body and sets unrealistic expectations for both men and women. In our culture, the objectification of women has been occurring for a while. Recent developments have shown the objectification of men as well. Given the cultural emphasis on unrealistic body images, the negative messages both genders face are tremendous. The role of sexually explicit material also raises concerns because of the impact it has in shaping people's view of their bodies. The Internet's ability to churn out body-perfect images amplifies these concerns. We hear significant numbers of stories about clients struggling with accepting their own body image, as well as the body image of their partner. The concept of "harvesting" is related to the infinite search for the picture of the perfect body. In a few cases these unrealistic expectations can contribute to sexual functioning concerns. Intrinsic in the online cultural messages we receive is the idea that sex is limited to youth, that older folks should not be sexual. Other negative thoughts we may have about ourselves as a result of cultural messages include, "My penis is too small," and "My breasts aren't OK."

Researchers examine factors contributing to body image struggles. Research suggests that a person's self-image is linked to the partner's response. Negative reactions from partners led to increased struggles with body image. As one could guess, individuals who struggle with body image issues have a better response to treatment progress when they have the support of a primary romantic partner. Individuals who receive such support have less stress and anxiety.

There are three implications that are important. First, for individuals who struggle with body image issues, the key is to gain support from the primary partner. Second, if the partner isn't supportive, it is important to address the negative impact of the partner's behavior; hearing "You're fat" isn't going to help individuals address body image. Third, partners are also pummeled by the same cultural messages. Partners may need training and education as well as feedback regarding providing the necessary support.

Much of this appears to be common sense. Explicit positive and negative messages about a person's body can easily be recognized for what they are. The difficulty, however, lies is recognizing implicit, hidden, or subtle positive or negative messages. For individuals struggling with sexual health concerns, assessing the messages you see from your online behavior is important.

While a lot of people struggle with obtaining the ideal body, as dictated by their culture, a mental health diagnosis reflects significant body image issues (see Cross Compulsivity/Eating disorder, page 67). Body Dysmorphic Disorder is characterized by constantly comparing your appearance with that of others, possibly refusing to let your picture be taken, excessive checking of a certain body part that you think is flawed (e.g., your nose or belly), feeling anxious and self-conscious around other people, calling yourself names or having plastic surgery and then feeling dissatisfaction with the results of plastic surgery. If this is an issue, please work with a mental health professional.

Developing a Healthy Body Image

Following are some guidelines that can help you work toward a positive body image:[15]

- Listen to your body. Eat when you are hungry.

- Be realistic about the size you are likely to be based on your genetic and environmental history.

- Exercise regularly in an enjoyable way, regardless of your size.

- Expect normal weekly and monthly changes in weight and shape.

- Work toward self-acceptance and self-forgiveness — be gentle with yourself.

- Ask for support and encouragement from friends and family when life is stressful.

- Decide how you wish to spend your energy — pursuing the "perfect body" or enjoying family, friends, school and, most importantly, life?

Assignment

- Review the discussion on Sexual Explicit Material (see page 141). How do images in online sexually explicit media shape your image of the human body? How do they shape how you see your body?

- How do images from online sexually explicit media shape how you see your partner's body?

- Examine your sexual history. How have messages regarding body image affected your sexual behavior?

- How have these messages led to increased online sexual behavior?

- How have these messages led to avoidant behaviors?

- List 25 negative thoughts you have about your body or hear from your culture(s). The goal is to help you become aware of the amount of negative self-talk.

- Next, for each negative message, review and investigate the source of the message. Was it the TV, family, culture, or other culture? Identify positive messages to balance the negative messages.

- Describe a realistic and healthy body image for you.

- Identify two plans you will do to create a healthy body image?

  -

  -

Fantasy and Masturbation

This section will examine two related topics of masturbation and fantasy. Both plan a primary role in the concept of cybersex. It is important to develop healthy approaches to both by addressing myths as well as examining the underlying values.

Masturbation

American culture has a significant amount of negative beliefs regarding masturbation. An article that presents the basics and history of masturbation is at Wikipedia (http://en.wikipedia.org/wiki/Masturbation). The focus of this section is to examine the role of masturbation in your sexual life. It is also important to examine your thoughts and the historical messages you have received about masturbation and to examine how these thoughts have helped or hindered your sexual health.

Respond to the following statements:

1. I enjoy masturbating.   YES / NO

2. Masturbation is a good way to affirm my sexuality.   YES / NO

3. Masturbation is a good way to help me feel better about myself.   YES / NO

4. I believe masturbation is sinful.   YES / NO

5. Masturbation is a healthy way to have sex when I'm horny.   YES / NO

6. Masturbation is a good way to get to know what a sexual partner likes.   YES / NO

7. Masturbation with my sexual partner(s) is a healthy expression of being close to each another.   YES / NO

8. Masturbation is very safe sex.   YES / NO

9. Masturbation is a healthy way to learn about my sexual desires.   YES / NO

10. Masturbation is a positive source of comfort and pleasure.   YES / NO

11. Masturbation is a form of healthy sexual expression.   YES / NO

12. Masturbation can be helpful in overcoming sexual dysfunction.   YES / NO

13. I masturbate to explore my body.   YES / NO

14. I masturbate too much.   YES / NO

15. I feel guilty when I masturbate.   YES / NO

16. Masturbation is a good way to reduce stress.   YES / NO

17. Masturbation is a good form of birth control.   YES / NO

Score 1 point for each "yes" response to statements 1–3, 5–13 and 16–17. Score 1 point for each "no" response to statements 4, 14, 15. The higher your score, the more comfortable you are with masturbation.

The questions above are a good place to start in assessing your views about masturbation. Review each question again, giving attention to your reaction. Review your sex history and the questions about masturbation. As you examine the responses, pay attention to your past and current thoughts and feelings about masturbation. For some people, masturbation is a form of harm reduction. By masturbating, they know they will reduce the risk of other sexual health problems.

One of the major concerns in treatment is the need to assess the role of the Internet and the linkage with sexual media and masturbation. The classic image of a guy masturbating to porn is the frequent archetype of Internet compulsivity. Often partners will have different opinions in addressing masturbation. Some say that masturbation is a healthy outlet within a relationship and that it should be incorporated into the relationship with their partner. Masturbation can be a way to discover what you like sexually, as well as what parts of your body are most arousing or sensitive. In this example, masturbation can lead to a heightened awareness of self that can be shared with your partner. In other opinions, masturbation is a form of settling when the primary partner is unavailable. One example is a guideline within a relationship where you ask the partner if he/she is available for sex. If the partner says, "no," then masturbation is allowed. Still other approaches view masturbation as a sin.

The key to the following questions is to clarify your opinions, beliefs and values about masturbation. Consider how the Internet has impacted these values. Think about the role of masturbation in your definition of sexual health.

Assignment

- Review the discussion on Culture (see page 77). Identify 2 messages about masturbation from each culture you belong to.

- What are my current values toward masturbation and fantasy?

- Describe the relationship between masturbation and your online sexual behavior.

- Describe the content and format of online material you've used while masturbating. Explain if this is healthy or unhealthy.

- Under what circumstances is masturbation healthy for you?

- Under what circumstances is masturbation unhealthy for you?

- What are my current appropriate masturbation behaviors? (Where, when, how often?)

- What are my guidelines about disclosing my masturbation behaviors to my partner?

• What is my partner's reaction to these guidelines?

Fantasy

Respond to the following statements:

1. If I fantasize about sex, I will become obsessed about sexual thoughts.   YES / NO
2. It is difficult for me to share my sexual fantasies with my sexual partner(s).   YES / NO
3. Sharing a sexual fantasy with my sexual partner(s) enriches my sex life.   YES / NO
4. Sexual fantasy helps me learn about what I like and don't like sexually.   YES / NO
5. Sharing a sexual fantasy is a good way to get to know what a sexual partner likes.   YES / NO
6. I enjoy fantasizing about sex.   YES / NO
7. I feel guilty when I fantasize about sex.   YES / NO
8. I enjoy hearing about my sexual partner's sexual fantasies.   YES / NO
9. Sexual fantasy helps me express my sexual desires.   YES / NO
10. Sexual fantasy is a safe outlet for sexual behaviors I choose not to act on.   YES / NO

Score 1 point for each "yes" response for statements 3–6 and 9–10. Score 1 point for each "no" response for statements 1, 2 and 8. The higher your score, the more comfortable you are with sexual fantasies.

The idea of sexual fantasies has many negative societal biases and messages that need to be confronted. In moving toward sexual health, it is important to clarify misperceptions that exist about fantasies. Having fantasies does not mean you are "oversexed," even if you fantasize or think about sex often.

Generally speaking, fantasies are normal aspects of our sexuality. Everybody has fantasies and daydreams. ***All*** of your Internet behavior is based on fantasy! Seriously, we cannot stress enough that all of you online behavior is related to fantasy. Given the conduit, all of the chat, pictures, and experiences exist in a realm where the mind has to fill in the blanks to make the experience feel real. Often online sexual behaviors lead to such intense fantasies that the fantasies take on an obsessive quality leading to the exclusion of real face-to-face intimacy. We have experienced significant numbers of clients who struggle with the ability to connect in a real-time face-to-face encounter due to the imbalance with Internet sexual compulsivity.

Fantasies themselves are neutral. They are normal and healthy. At the same time, it is important to emphasize that some fantasies are risky or unhealthy. For some, the Internet has led to such an imbalance, significant therapy needs to focus on addressing the fantasy content. The content, frequency, intensity and focus of the fantasy may raise issues you need to address. Fantasies can be helpful in understanding your sexuality. By examining your fantasies you can get a sense of what you find arousing. You can understand your needs and share them with your partner and support network. Sometimes a person can channel his or her energy into sexual fantasies to allow a healthy release. Sharing fantasies is difficult for some people, yet the process of sharing your fantasies can create positive intimacy with your partner.

Sexual fantasies are thoughts and feelings about sexual behaviors and ideas we find sexually arousing. Sexual fantasies may represent what turns us on. Sexual fantasies are also a form of self-stimulation. Simply having a fantasy does not mean we have to act on that fantasy. Fantasies exist only in thoughts; they are not in themselves real. This also means that a fantasy about a negative traumatic event is also not real.

We distinguish between a sexualization and a sexual fantasy by using a "three-second rule." The three-second rule refers to the amount of time you think about a person. What transforms a sexualization into a sexual fantasy is the thought or fixation on a particular person, image or object. If the thought is less than three seconds, it is a sexualization. If it is longer than 3 seconds, it is a fantasy.

We came up with the three-second rule in response to clients asking for a helpful guideline on when the process switches from a sexualization to a fantasy. We base this rule on clinical experience and not necessarily on any hard and fast research. Nor does it have to be three seconds: it could be two or four seconds.

Sexualizations are normal, they happen outside our realm of control and they're part of our sexual drive. Sexualizations simply happen. Throughout the day, many sexualizations occur. A sexualization is recognition that someone is attractive to you. Often sexualizations can occur outside one's primary sexual partner template. A straight man can recognize a handsome guy, just as a gay man can recognize a beautiful woman. In these situations, there is simply recognition of the sexuality and sensuality of another person. It is our response to the sexualization that raises issues for further treatment.

If a person uses sexual fantasies to avoid or escape from reality, or the fantasies are one's only form of sexual expression, then we have some concern. Some clients have used fantasies as a form of escape from unpleasant thoughts and feelings. The key is for you to figure out which fantasies are healthy and which are unhealthy.

Occasionally, thoughts of inappropriate or unhealthy behaviors may occur as themes in your fantasies. This is an important issue for individuals with a pattern of sexually offending behavior. It is also true for people in chemical dependency recovery when sexual fantasies include drug use. How you respond to the unhealthy fantasies is a key step toward sexual health. You can redirect and change the fantasy through changing the "plot" of the fantasy. If you find that you cannot do this, it is important that you stop the fantasy and avoid actively encouraging the unhealthy fantasy. Changing your environment and talking with your network can help you avoid these unhealthy fantasies. It is important that you not masturbate to these fantasies, because you might make them stronger or more frequent. If you recognize that unhealthy fantasies are increasing in frequency, intensity or content, you could be in a high-risk situation. Letting your support system know you're having unhealthy or risky fantasies can be a part of your prevention plan.

In our fantasies, we can create and clarify our values regarding sexuality and our relationship with others. Jack Morin identifies the concept of "core erotic thought," which he uses to demonstrate how our thoughts shape our sexual fantasies. Examining our most powerful fantasies gives us insight into how we see our basic selves. In his book, *Erotic Mind*, Morin discusses how fantasies changed in light of the therapeutic process. Specifically, he describes how negative and damaging fantasies slowly decrease as clients address underlying issues. As the clients move toward health, Morin suggests that the fantasies changed as a result of the therapeutic work. The goal for this section is to emphasize not only the importance of acknowledging the fantasies, but also the importance of studying them in order to gain insight into our underlying patterns of thinking and move toward sexual health. Assessing the role of the Internet is a part of this process as well. Consider the following possibilities: Fantasies may be a form of online harm –reduction. Fantasies may be a form of alternative sexual expression. Or, fantasies may be a form of avoidance. You need to clarify the role of fantasy in your life.

Assignment

- Identify three highly arousing fantasies you've had recently. In a separate notebook, write 2-3 pages per fantasy with as much detail as possible. Complete a behavioral analysis on the fantasy (see page 71). Consider the following questions:

- What is the content of the fantasy? Explain the five "Ws": who, what, when, why, where.

- How is the Internet related to each of the fantasies? Consider images, themes, thoughts, feelings, or individuals that are connected to the Internet.

- If this fantasy were to become a reality what would you think and feel as a result?

- Examine the role of the Internet in your fantasies. Describe the use, content, and form of online behavior linked with your fantasies. Assess if this is healthy or unhealthy.

Sexually Explicit Material

One of the more controversial issues in the field of sexual health is the role and use of sexually explicit material (we describe this below). Notice the language: we use the phrase "sexual explicit material" to describe any content used in a sexual manner instead of using the problematic term "pornography." (Pornography is often assumed to be limited to nude magazines or nude videos.) We use this approach for two reasons. One reason for the change in language is to step beyond the controversy of the language, and second highlight the need to assess adequately the use of ANY material a person sees as sexually explicit or might use in a sexually stimulating way.

The shear number of explicit images of all kinds on the Internet is phenomenal. As we saw in the section on body image, Internet images shape our view of what we find attractive. In the previous section on fantasy, Internet images can also have a profound impact. Sexually explicit material includes sex images, but it also includes benign advertisements such as images from catalogs, storefronts or billboards. The number of clients who report they looked at bra ads while growing up demonstrates how material can be sexually explicit without being pornographic. Some find the models in Victoria's Secret and Abercrombie & Fitch advertising sexually arousing. Or, likewise, Men's Health magazine or the Sports Illustrated swimsuit issue. Although these images are not nude, people do use them for sexual purposes, including masturbation and fantasy.

Experts have differing opinions on the use of sexually explicit material. Some clinicians believe any and all sexually explicit material is unhealthy because it exploits others and can be misused. Some religious traditions believe that looking at sexually explicit material is tantamount to infidelity and therefore is a sin (equivalent to "coveting your neighbor's wife"). Other clinicians have a neutral reaction to the use of sexually explicit material and focus on the surrounding context. Still other clinicians use sexually explicit material to educate couples and to help them address sexual functioning issues and facilitate the sharing of sexual thoughts with a partner. For the sake of this exercise, we define "sexually explicit" as any material you use for sexual arousal or which you sexualize (see the section on Fantasy on page 137).

The role of sexually explicit material in your life plays a part in your sexual health. Our approach is to help you identify your current use of sexually explicit material, review your values regarding the material and focus on the role of the material in your sexual health. Taking on the values that (you think) others hold – or what you think they want you to hold – only sets you up for failure. Frequently, we have worked with clients who present as having an Internet problem, because their partner objects to sexually explicit material.

Assignment

Review your sex history and timeline; identify the type and amount of sexually explicit material you've used both online and offline. As you increase your awareness of the type and amount of material, also focus on what you find arousing or attractive. As mentioned, the content can range from pictures, videos, online materials, stories, advertising material and even art. As a starting point in your personal assessment, begin with an extremely conservative definition of sexually explicit material. Note any medium with content you sexualize. Focus on how much material you explicitly seek out versus material simply present in your environment. The key is to become aware of the degree to which sexual content is present in your life.

• What online sexually explicit material have you used?

• What offline sexually explicit material have you used?

• Describe how you have used this material.

- What are my current values toward sexually explicit material?

- What online sexually explicit material is acceptable to use? Why?

- What online sexually explicit material is acceptable to use? Why?

- What sexually explicit material is not acceptable to use? Why?

- What are your guidelines about disclosing your use of sexually explicit material to my partner?

- Have you reviewed these guidelines with your partner? Does your partner agree with these values? If there is disagreement, what is your plan to address the disagreement?

Positive Sexuality

In this section, we turn the discussion upside down. In previous sections, we focused on factors associated with acting-out behaviors; here we reshape the conversation to help you think about what you want. Here we want to you focus on what is right versus what is wrong. As we have said, all behavior is goal focused. How do you get your sexual needs met in a healthy way? And, what is the role of the Internet in meeting those sexual needs in a healthy way? Such questions are the focus of this section.

What is Positive Sexuality?

To understand positive sexuality, first we must understand sexuality in a brand new way – as a normal, vital, and positive aspect of your life. Too many people suffer pain when they think about sexuality. Give yourself permission to be a sexual being. Rather than repressed, hidden or shamed, positive sexuality celebrates your sexual energy and being. Yes, this includes sexual behavior, but it includes much more.

The key to this section is discovery. If you watched a child in a playground, you would see her meandering through all of the play areas. She might stop at the swings, or the merry-go-round. Next, she might check out the slide. Then, perhaps she might build something in the sand. When she likes something, the child stays in the area. So, too, is the role of discovery in the realm of sexuality. Sex is adult play, so check out what you like or don't like. Enjoy the positive experiences, and let go of the unpleasant experiences. Pay attention to what energizes you, makes you feel alive, leaves you light-hearted, reflects integrity in your life, and can be shared with your support network. The Internet is a tool. Ask yourself how this tool can facilitate positive sexuality. In some cases, the Internet will be helpful. In other cases, the Internet has such a negative pull that it isn't possible to be helpful.

Your task in this section is to challenge most, if not all of the messages you have heard about sexuality. This doesn't mean you have to discard your beliefs. Instead, understand both the letter and spirit of the messages. Sexual health is a journey. Today's thoughts are for today. What you like today is for today. What you want is for today. You have the privilege of addressing tomorrow's likes and wants tomorrow.

Balance is important in the journey. You can change your mind on this journey. We place good/bad sexual experiences on a different continuum than the continuum of healthy/unhealthy. You can have a sexual encounter that feels good but is unhealthy (think meth/sex), and a bad experience that is healthy (think too tired to function, but emotional intimacy). Our hope is that you have great experiences along the way. Sometimes, the only way we know what is sweet is because we can compare it to what is sour. Enjoy your journey in sexual health!

The rest of the topics in Stage Two will focus on topics important in developing sexual skills and creating the healthy encounters on your journey.

Assertive Communication

In moving toward sexual health, it is important to develop assertive communication skills while avoiding passive, aggressive and passive/aggressive communication patterns. This is relevant not only to expressing thoughts and feelings but also relevant to expressing yourself sexually. It is important to communicate with your partners your sexual likes and needs. At first, this style of communication may feel artificial. We encourage you to view it as a template and helpful tool. There are many formulas that can be helpful in learning assertive communication. We like the following template:

1. I am committed to__(a few words on why you are doing this)___.

2. I think/I feel____(state your thought or feeling).

3. Because____(explain what triggered the thought or feeling).

4. I need/want/would like___(express the request).

5. I commit to__(identify how you will help this person be successful)__.

Each statement has its own purpose for developing a stronger relationship and eventually helping you get your needs met.

In statement #1, think about the times when you've received helpful feedback. Typically you trusted that or knew these people were on your side. Reminding your listener of your goal helps them understand that the assertive communication is focused on growth: "In terms of a relationship, I'm committed to a loving relationship." Statement #2 is about being self-aware, about asking "What's going on inside?" It may be a thought, feeling or memory triggered by the current moment. Your ability to answer the question is improved by the mindfulness exercises (see page 46). Statement #3 should be a simple explanation of the moment, "short and sweet" and explicitly connected to the moment. If it takes more than one breath to say it, then it's too long. Statement #4 is a request, and the key is to be clear, specific and measurable. Again, if it takes more than one breath, then it is too long. Bear in mind distinctions among 'needs', 'wants' and 'likes'. Often, language confuses the importance of something. Someone says, "I *need* a cell phone," but in reality, they merely *want* or *would like* a cell phone. A need is a basic requirement for existence: "I need food," or "I need respect" or "I need you to stop touching me." Finally, Statement #5 declares how you will help the other person be successful, something you will do to support the goal. It can include such statements as, "I will tell you when I want to be touched," or, "I will tell you what I like instead of making you guess." Helping the person be successful reconnects you to Statement #1. The template builds the relationship.

There are a few pitfalls to avoid. First, it is important to avoid the passive approach toward communication. A classic danger is the phrase "Would you like to …?" instead of "I would like . . ." or "I expect …" Other unhelpful forms of communication are "We" statements. Use "I" statements instead. Equally important is to avoid aggressive communication, including the manner of the communication (i.e., loud, yelling) or language such as " You" statements which are often more aggressive. "You should . . ." is better replaced with "I want" or "I need."

It is important to consider how the Internet is related to assertive communication. We have worked with individuals who use the Internet to avoid assertive communication. Rather than ask or reach out to their partners, they avoid interactions. Rather than assertively express their needs, they resort to indirect ways to meet their needs.

Assertively expressing your requests is a significant component of sexual health. Setting boundaries and setting limits can have major impacts on relationships. Assertiveness is important in expressing feelings and sexual desires. We have provided only a brief introduction to the concept. If the topic is relevant to you, or if you have significant struggles with assertive communication, please follow up with your support network.

Assignment

- Examine your sexual history. How is the lack of assertiveness related to your behaviors?

- Identify times when you have engaged in passive, aggressive or passive/aggressive behaviors. How could you change these encounters into assertive communication?

- What is the role of thoughts and feelings in your ability to be assertive? Could shame (see page 84) be present? If you feel shame, you might be hesitant to ask for what you want or need.

- In light of the previous questions, describe the relationship between assertive communication and your use of the Internet.

- What are your plans to improve your assertiveness communication skills?

Boundaries

"Boundaries" refers to the limits we choose in life. It is the process of defining what is acceptable. Boundaries vary between individuals. You define your own boundaries.

Typically, we think of boundaries as being healthy, rigid or blurred. Healthy boundaries are well defined, clearly communicated and respectful to yourself and others. Healthy boundaries are an expression of our identity and although they can change, they generally are stable across time and situations. Changes in boundaries can occur in response to unique circumstances, the environment and people. Our personal experience can lead to a healthy expansion or restriction of a boundary. For example, if you are tired and lonely, a boundary may be that you will not have sex. But once you're in a relationship, given the same circumstances, you may choose to have sex with your partner because of the adult play aspect. While boundaries can change, you should view any rapid changes in your boundaries and limits as a warning sign.

Two types of unhealthy boundaries are blurred and rigid boundaries. They represent the opposite extremes of the spectrum (with healthy boundaries in the middle). Blurred boundaries are too flexible and too changeable. With blurred boundaries, we tend to let the outside environment or other people dictate our beliefs, values and limits. In this situation, we may feel used, violated, exposed and hurt. Our identity is lost. We've experience many clients who think they have a problem because their partner thinks they have a problem.

At the other extreme are rigid boundaries. Rigid boundaries often appear to be extreme stances. In substance-abuse treatment, we talk about an "all or nothing" way of thinking or a "take no prisoners" mentality. The consequences of the rigid boundaries are often isolation, loneliness and judgmentalism.

Three types of boundaries are worth focusing on: *physical, emotional* and *sexual.* Physical boundary is the space around us. When working with children, we use the idea of a "bubble space" surrounding us that intuitively helps children understand how close they can get to another person. The concept of a bubble space supports the idea that boundaries are flexible. Depending on the circumstances, the size of the bubble space changes. For example, we are more comfortable if someone sits next to us in a room full of people, as contrasted with the discomfort we feel when only two people are in the room. Depending on the person and the culture, the bubble space changes as well, and there are different rules on how close you can stand to someone. With friends and family members, our bubble space is smaller; with strangers, it's larger.

Emotional and intellectual boundaries reflect your right to your feelings and thoughts. We individuals have the right to our feelings and beliefs based on values, spirituality, education or cultural affiliation. Our emotional and intellectual boundaries define our personality and identity, and they are a major component in our sexual health. The key is to examine how your boundaries shape your sexual behaviors.

Sexual boundaries reflect your right to your feelings, thoughts and behaviors in the realm of sexuality. We individuals have the right to our feelings and beliefs based on values, spirituality, education or cultural affiliation. These boundaries are a major component in our sexual health. In a future assignment, you will define in detail what behaviors are healthy for you (see page 153).

A boundary violation occurs when someone deliberately or accidentally infringes on the limits of what we are comfortable with. A boundary is violated when you are touched when you do not want to be touched. An emotional boundary is violated when you are subjected to constant criticism, when someone reads another's mail or email without permission, when someone tells us what we should feel or think. The list of potential boundary violations is infinite. In some clients, unhealthy boundaries are a major issue in the recovery process. Using the following list of Warning Symptoms of Unhealthy Boundaries as a starting place, ask yourself whether any warning symptoms are present. If so, you might be able to trace the symptoms back to a possible boundary violation. Also, ask yourself how the warning symptoms might relate to your sexual health, and whether the Internet plays a role either in creating – or is a reaction to – the symptoms of unhealthy boundaries. If the Internet does play a role, identify a plan to address the concerns with your support network.

If present, identify a plan to address the concerns with your support network.

Warning Signs of Unhealthy Boundaries

- When you do not want sexual contact, but go along with it anyway so the person will like you.
- Telling someone you like a behavior when you don't.
- Saying you want to get together with someone when you don't.
- Using drugs in a sexual setting when you don't want to.
- Not expressing your sexual desires or preferences with a partner and simply going along with what they want.
- "Falling in love" with anyone who reaches out to you.
- Acting on a first sexual impulse even when you say you will wait until you know the person first.
- Using sex to express anger or loneliness.
- Being sexual for your partner, not yourself.
- Going against personal values to please others.
- Using the Internet as an escape.
- Not noticing when someone else shows poor boundaries.
- Touching a person without asking.
- Letting others tell you what you should or should not do.
- Letting others tell you what is and is not healthy sexual behavior.
- Expecting others to automatically know what you want.
- Engaging in unsafe sex when you say you will not.

Developing healthy boundaries is easier said than done. Learning boundaries is often through trial and error. There is no magic way to develop and express your boundaries. Identifying what you like and dislike is essential. Healthy boundaries are a function of assertive communication where you express your likes and dislikes. It is important that if you don't like something, it's something to communicate and place outside what is acceptable. If you like something, include it within your boundaries. It is your responsibility to express your boundaries to others. As a reminder, this topic serves as a complement to the discussions of Sexual Behavior and Expression (see page 151) and Assertive Communication (see page 145). Please review those discussions again in light of our discussion of Boundaries.

Assignment

- Review your sexual history and timeline. Pay attention to thoughts, feelings, experiences or behaviors that might be a possible boundary violation.

- Review your sexual history and timeline. Which of other people's boundaries might you have crossed?

- Review your Internet use. How has your Internet use contributed to your boundary violations of others?

- How has your Internet use been an attempt to cope with violations of your boundaries?

Sexual Behavior and Expression

Throughout history, there have been attempts to define sexually appropriate behavior. Within the Judeo-Christian tradition, for example, the "Holiness Code" of the early Israelites was an attempt to define healthy sexual behavior reflecting their values, knowledge and community goals. For a small nomadic people, sexually healthy behavior emphasized procreation. The society's patriarchal system viewed women as property, so most of the holiness code focused on male sexuality. For a society with limited information on biology, the Holiness Code attempted to identify sexually healthy behaviors as a function of blood and energy: loss of blood equaled loss of energy and reflected a threat to survival. As a consequence, women were to be avoided during their menstrual periods.

Fast forward 2000 years to a Europe dominated by the Romans with a new religion (i.e., Christianity) gradually extinguishing paganism. Hence, it was important to reject anything that reflected paganism, including the sexual component of the pagan traditions. Fast-forward another 2000 years – to today – and we have a society unlike any previous society, one that understands biology, genetics and multicultural reality. This reality leads to corresponding attempts at defining sexual behavior and a diversity of sexually healthy behaviors.

Obviously, none of the historical cultural definitions of healthy sexuality take into account the role of the Internet. We are living in unique times. As the Internet transforms the world, the corresponding definition of what is healthy needs to be clarified in the ever-changing balance between the individual and society.

Many of the historical attempts to define sexual healthy behaviors have emphasized actual sexual acts and condemned the behavior within the context of a religious statement ("This act is unhealthy; it is a sin"). As a result, these definitions are bound by culture and time. Too often clients are stuck in the trap of asking the "expert" to define what he or she should do. Too often, based on their worldview, clinicians are ready to proclaim what is healthy and what is not.

In the last thirty-five years, experts in the field of human sexuality have attempted to define sexual health. The definition of sexual health used in this book reflects that research and development. While not reviewed here, the process of defining sexual health has experienced multiple revisions, discussions and bumps along the way. At one point, scholars argued that a universal definition was not possible given the diversity of people, sexualities, cultures, and circumstances. More recent attempts have attempted to facilitate an interaction between the individual and culture by incorporating a dynamic feedback process in clarifying sexually healthy behaviors. The goal is to help you start thinking about the values that shape your life. As you begin to identify these values, your responsibility is to assess the consistency between these values and your online and offline behaviors. This is not a do-it-yourself, go-it-alone, I-can-do-anything-I-want task.

You need your support network. It reflects the community and it is there to provide support, encouragement and accountability.

Unhealthy Sexual Behaviors

The consensus among experts in a variety of fields (medicine, mental health, child welfare and clergy) is that only one behavior has consistently been defined as unhealthy: sexual behavior that is exploitive or done without consent. For example, exploitation of children is one of the few universally consistent behaviors condemned across time and across cultures. Yet, even this example has gray areas. In modern America, the definition of a child who can give legal consent for sexual contact ranges from age 14 to age 18. Centuries ago, it was not uncommon for a 12-year-old girl who had just completed puberty (i.e., had a period) to be considered an adult. Today, our collective culture would define this as abuse. Another gray area is exploitation. Activists working against the pornography industry argue that the material exploits women. If so, how does one explain gay pornography? These gray areas highlight the danger and difficulty of universal declarations.

An example sure to raise hackles is the assertion (by a significant group of people) suggesting that sexual behavior focused on procreation within marriage is the only form of healthy sex, that any sex act that isn't open to procreation, even within a marriage, is a sin. This approach denounces as sin any form of masturbation or use of pornography. Online sexual behavior is therefore a sin because it doesn't lead to procreation. Some people have modified this approach to emphasize that any sex within marriage is healthy. Still others further modify this approach, believing that any consensual sex within marriage is healthy, recognizing that some traditions emphasize the wife's religious duty to submit to her husband.

Recently, there has been a push within the Lesbian, Gay, Bisexual and Transgender (LGBT) community to emphasize monogamy as the only form of healthy sexual expression and the need for marriage rights as a validation of these healthy behaviors. Sadly, where to draw the line of healthy vs. unhealthy sexual behavior seems to depend on what side of the line you fall on. If you are "outside" the line, you redraw the line to include your sexual behaviors. Given the relative newness of the Internet, there is a corresponding development in defining healthy online behaviors.

Healthy Sexual Behaviors

The approach taken in this workbook emphasizes a dynamic process between the community and the individual. Your values determine what behaviors are healthy for you and define what is a healthy use of the Internet. However, this is not a free-for-all. Part of the process includes disclosure and community conversations within your support network to review your continuing care plan. As part of Stage Three, you will identify values and sexual behaviors that are congruent and that reflect your personal definition of sexual health. The role of the Internet will be reviewed in light of the impact it has on your personal definition of sexual health. The following is a presentation of four values that are helpful in defining healthy sexual behaviors. Depending on your reaction to any behavior, you choose to put behavior in YOUR unhealthy or healthy column.

Four values helpful in defining healthy sexual behaviors

Life Giving

The offline or online sexual behavior is a positive aspect in your life. This value of sexual behavior is that the experience makes you feel alive and energized. Your personal identity (and your partner's) is affirmed, created and even expanded. You can walk away from the experience with your head held high. There is a sense of fulfillment and even pride in the experience. While life giving, this does not necessarily mean the experience is limited to "great sex" but rather there is an enhancement of identity and personhood for those involved. Sexual behavior is sometimes referred to as "adult play," suggesting a sense of fun, playfulness, and timelessness.

Open and Honest

Healthy sexual behavior is above board, open, and honest. While you may not talk about the incident with everyone because of discretion, you could disclose the online activity to your support network. In disclosing to your support network, its members would respond that the behavior is consistent with your declared values and continuing care plan. Not being open and honest is an immediate red flag.

Consent

Full consent and awareness are present in the encounters. Consent implies that all partners are actively giving permission to engage in the online behavior, in other words, your not keeping secrets from your support network. Consent requires appropriate disclosures and considerations. If you use the Internet to hook up with someone in real time, this value assumes that full disclosure has occurred with your partner, including risks for STI's, pregnancy, relationship status/availability or statuses your partner should be aware of if the behavior occurs in the real world. There is a decided lack of manipulation in the experience. (An example of manipulation is saying, "If you love me, you would have sex with me.")

In some circumstances, consent is not possible. Children are not able to give consent. Relationships with power differences (for example, student/teacher, boss/employee, and therapist/client) are by definition non-consensual. Other circumstances exist where the ability to give consent is questionable because of mental health issues, chemical use or financial status (e.g., "survival sex," where one trades sex for shelter). Another notion embodied within consent is that all parties need to be aware of the experience, which is why exhibitionism and voyeurism are unhealthy - and illegal.

Finally, within the concept of consent is the concept of respect for the partner's boundaries and limits. If consent is removed (i.e., one partner saying "Stop," "No," "I don't want to"), the behavior must stop. Any person can remove consent at any time, with or without a reason.

Responsibility

As a value, Responsibility requires that you ultimately assert fully your sexual needs, likes and dislikes. How are you protecting your values? Are the limits you're agreeing to truly yours? Or are they limits you think are necessary because someone else wants you to have them? It is up to you – not the other person – to affirm, communicate and protect your values

Assignment

The following assignment is based on the concept that sexual energy is healthy, and that when it is channeled in healthy ways, it can bring new life and strengthen relationships. Your responses should be harmonious with your values.

Part 1: Review the sex history assignment on page 24. Use this list as a starting point; consider how many of these behaviors are consistent with the four values above in your life. If they are not, remove them from your list of sexually healthy behaviors. Anything that remains is a candidate for a healthy behavior.

Part 2: Answer the following questions.

• Who is an appropriate sexual partner for you (age, sex, relationship, etc.)?

• What types of sexual behaviors are healthy for you?

• What types of sexual behavior should you avoid?

• When is it appropriate to be sexually active for you?

• Where is it appropriate to be sexually active for you?

• What are healthy reasons to engage in sexual behavior for you?

- What are unhealthy reasons to engage in sexual behavior for you?

- What are healthy reasons to engage in online sexual behaviors for you?

- What are unhealthy reasons to engage in online sexual behavior for you?

- What kind of online behaviors are acceptable for you?

- What kind of online behaviors are unacceptable for you?

- How will you communicate these responses to your partner?

- What do I need to learn about my primary partner to help my primary partner experience sexual health?

Intimacy and Relationships

The majority of most people's life energy is focused on developing connections. This is true regarding online behavior. One of the major causes of online sexual behavior is the belief that it will produce a sense of intimacy, yet, ironically, one of the major consequences is the destruction of intimacy. In this section, our goal is to help you become aware of the types of intimacy that are important to you, strategize on getting these intimacy needs met and eventually develop the type of relationships that you want.

Desire for Intimacy

One of the best definitions of intimacy is "the feeling of connection with another person. Intimacy is the soul-to-soul connection between two people. Intimacy is a connection with openness and honesty." To expand our understanding of intimacy, it is helpful to review different types of intimacy.

The need or desire to connect with others is healthy and normal. Most of the memorable moments in our lives are about the experience of intimacy. Similarly, most of the painful memories are about the loss of intimacy. If we look at the present moment, there are many types of intimate connections occurring all the time. Each moment of life is a possible connection to another person. Each moment of life is an experience of intimacy. If we limit our ability to see these intimate connections, then we limit our ability to experience intimacy. The question to consider is "How am I connected to the person next to me at this time?"

Below, we examine twelve different types of intimacy that have been identified by researchers.[16] After you review the various types of intimacy, next think about how to build intimacy in your life. Under each type of intimacy are suggestions for enhancing your intimacy skills in that area. But they are not the only ways or necessarily the "correct" ways. Use what works for you or develop other ideas.

Types of Intimacy

There are a variety of definitions for intimacy. One of the best definitions of intimacy is "the feeling of connection with another person. Intimacy is the soul-to-soul connection between two people. Intimacy is a connection with openness and honesty." To expand our understanding of intimacy, it is helpful to review different types of intimacy.

The need or desire to connect with others is healthy and normal. Most of the highlights in our life are about the experience of intimacy. Similarly, most of the painful memories are about the loss of intimacy. If we look at the present moment, there are many types of intimate connections occurring all the time. Each moment of life is a possible connection to another person. Each moment of life is an experience of intimacy. To limit our ability to see these intimate connections limits our ability to experience intimacy. The question to consider is "How am I connected to the person next to me at this time?"

Once you have reviewed the types of intimacy, the next step is to highlight how to build intimacy in your life. Under each type of intimacy are suggestions on what you might do to enhance your intimacy skills in each area. Use what works for you or develop other ideas. They are far from the only way or the correct way.

Emotional Intimacy

Emotional intimacy is the sharing of significant experiences and feelings. Emotional intimacy is the foundation of all other forms of intimacy. It is the ability to talk without fear. Anything you are afraid of talking about is a possible moment of transformation of fear into intimacy. When fear is present, talking about it can facilitate a stronger and closer relationship. Emotional intimacy includes the ability to share one's hopes and dreams.

- Through therapy, examine life events that have hindered your ability to be in a relationship. These issues might be grief, abuse and/or fear. Share these examples with your support network.

- Read a self-help book. This type of book will help you start to identify and cope with feelings and emotions. Visit a local bookstore and examine titles that speak to you.

- Appropriately share your inner thoughts, feelings, desires and needs with other people in your life.

- Find a support group. Pick a group, such as AA or another program, that addresses an important issue in your life. A wide range of topics exist that may fit your concerns. You'll get a lot of experience sharing your feelings, thoughts, dreams and struggles.

Sexual Intimacy

Sexual intimacy is more than just the physical act of sex. Talking about the deepest and darkest sexual secrets is a form of sexual intimacy. For some of our clients, we are the first individuals they talk to about sexuality.

- Attend a workshop on sexuality.

- Share your fantasies with your partner.

- Strategize with your partner about how to make a part (or all) of a fantasy come true (within the rules of your relationship).

- Read a book on sexuality and share with your partner what you liked and disliked.

- Share your work from this workbook with others (as appropriate). Examine how your online behavior was related to sexual intimacy. Develop plans to get these needs met in ways that are consistent with your life values.

Intellectual Intimacy

Intellectual intimacy is the closeness resulting from sharing ideas. There is a genuine respect for each person's opinion. Agreement on a topic is not required for intellectual intimacy. The process of sharing, reflecting and discussing highlights the aspects of intellectual intimacy.

- Take a class. Check out community colleges, local art groups and area newspapers for classes that may interest you.

- Teach a course.

- Start a book club.

- Join a listserv on a topic of your choice.

- Check out the Internet blogs on a topic of your choice.

Aesthetic Intimacy

Aesthetic intimacy relates to experiences of beauty. This can include expressions of art such as music, plays and movies but also natural beauty such as sunrises, listening to a thunderstorm, and taking a day hike.

- Beauty is definitely in the eye of the beholder, so what do you find beautiful? After you have figured it out, seek it out.

- If you like art, visit a museum, an art space, a play or a movie.

- Love nature? Check out local hiking or outdoor groups to join.

- Missed your shot at "American Idol?" How about joining a local chorus?

- Traditional art not your thing? Walk through your city and photograph graffiti you find interesting. Seek out information regarding body art (tattoos).

- Peruse non-X or R rated Internet sites such as Flickr.

Creative Intimacy

Creative intimacy is the intimacy of shared discovery. The key component is the process of co-creating with another person. Both you and the other person can grow in deeper ways through the experience.

- Bring a friend with you to any activity you enjoy and would like to share.

- Join an art class.

- Read a book on "possibility," such as the *Power of Now* by Eckhart Tolle, or *Power of Intention* by William Dwyer

Recreational Intimacy

Recreational intimacy refers to the experience of play, stepping beyond the struggles of life and simply spending time together. The types of play include sports, outdoor activities and indoor activities. Sometimes other types of intimacies are incorporated into recreational activities, such as going to a movie (aesthetic) and then talking about it afterward (intellectual).

- Go to the gym, walk or engage in other physical activities.

- Find a club or group to join. For example, most cities have hobby or recreation groups such as bowling or volleyball. Do what you enjoy regardless of what others think. You might be surprised how many people share your interests.

Work Intimacy

Work intimacy occurs in the sharing of tasks. It can include projects, events or the process of long-term commitment regarding work or family. These tasks vary in type, intensity and duration and could include completing a project at work or cleaning up the house. The feeling of satisfaction when completing a task with another person is an example of work intimacy.

- Volunteer for work events or tasks. Join a committee at work.

- Talk with your co-workers about what is going on. As appropriate, ask them what they did last night or over the weekend. Start sharing the basics with them as well.

- Volunteer for organizations or events that are close to your heart. These could be community activities such as a festival or a political campaign.

Crisis Intimacy

Crisis intimacy occurs because of major and minor tragedies. Personal crises may be illness or accidents. Larger forms of crisis intimacy can be community experiences of a natural disaster. In these situations, people step outside of their limits and connect. Strangers will go beyond typical behaviors. The long-term response of the gay community to HIV is a great example of this type of intimacy. The community response to breast cancer is another example.

- Volunteer for a cause that you think is important. This could include rescue missions, food drives and cleanup duty.

- Learn from the crisis and develop long-term safety plans.

Commitment Intimacy

Commitment intimacy is the experience of hope and possibility in response to addressing an issue, cause or event bigger than one individual. This can range from a short-term task (completing a social service project) to a never-ending task such as social justice. It is the process of transforming the world.

- Identify a cause or value that means something to you. Volunteer your time, talent or treasure.

- Within the 12-step tradition, service work is about commitment intimacy.

Spiritual Intimacy

Spiritual intimacy develops through sharing the most important areas of concerns including values, meaning of life and the core of our being. It is an experience of possibility and transcendence beyond the daily experience of who we are. It can include religious traditions and practices, but ultimately it is about how we connect with personal meaning (Or, God, in whatever way you understand God).

- Talk to a spiritual advisor of a group different from the one you grew up.

- Join a church.

- Join a 12-step group. This could be AA but it might also be a 12-step group for partners of AA, Internet sexual compulsivity, debtors, eating and even "Emotions Anonymous."

- Join an online group that discusses life values.

Communication Intimacy

Communication intimacy is the process of full disclosure with another person. It is the process of being open, honest and truthful. This includes giving difficult and constructive feedback, even when it's not easy to do so.

- Simply say what you mean, and mean what you say. (Too often, people say what they think other people want to hear.)

- Learn how to be present and listen to other people by attending a listening training program.

- Continue to share insights into your progress with your support network.

Conflict Intimacy

Conflict intimacy is the process of connecting and respectful fighting, as well as facing differences with others and struggling to understand one another. There is a sense of closeness that transcends conflict and ultimately leads to a closer relationship. The power of "make-up sex" highlights how conflict intimacy is so powerful.

- Recognize that healthy fighting is a normal part of a relationship.

- Learn how to fight in healthy ways by reading a book on conflict management/resolution, such as *The Eight Essential Steps to Conflict Resolution.*

- Attend an anger-management course.

- Attend a problem-solving course or read problem-solving material online.

These 12 types of intimacy are simply a place to start. They are not exclusive, or exhaustive. Instead, they are designed to help you start thinking of what you want in your life, and how to start getting the needs met in healthy ways. Review your online behavior in light of a need for intimacy. How have you coped with, damaged, or otherwise tried to get these needs met?

Touch/Physical Intimacy

Touch/Physical Intimacy (or Touch Needs) is a form of physical intimacy requiring special focus. The overlap between sexual intimacy and touch intimacy leads to significant confusion. Classic social psychology research has suggested that the failure to receive touch can have a severe negative health, social and emotional impact on a person. The types of touch exist on a continuum. Nurturing touch is healthy and is expressive of a relationship. Touching people is one way of reaching out and affirming them – and being affirmed yourself.

Unhealthy touch is the opposite. Exploitive touch is manipulative, forced or unwanted. It can be a way to express hurt, anger or fear. Some touch is confusing; it occurs in the middle or grey area of the touch continuum. In this confusing center are experiences of touch that appear healthy but leave a person unsure about the intent. Examples may be a hug that includes a brush against breasts, buttocks or genitalia, or a kiss that goes on too long. In moving toward sexual health, it is important to recognize healthy and unhealthy touch and to identify ways to get your touch needs met. You may also want to review the topic on abuse (see page 115).

In modern American culture, there is a significant barrier to touch. So many of the messages about touch actually sexualize touch. As a result, we may misinterpret the messages of another person. In America, two guys holding hands are seen as a gay couple rather than two friends together, different from the way these two would be viewed in many Middle Eastern cultures. There are also gender differences. Touch is culturally encouraged for many women, but not for men. The typical woman has a better understanding of touch needs than the typical man. The misunderstanding of touch raises significant problems regarding sexual harassment claims. In sexualizing touch, our culture has deprived us of ways to get healthy needs met in appropriate ways. This misunderstanding can lead to miscommunication, conflicts and resentments in sexual, social and emotional relationships.

In developing ways to get your touch needs meet, it is also important to be clear about your motivation. In reviewing your online sexual behavior, how many times have you engaged in the behavior when what you were looking for was simply affirmation through touch?

Barriers to Intimacy

Barriers to intimacy can be internal or external. Internal barriers reflect issues in our life and our interaction with others. They may be historical (history of abuse) or current (shame or depression). These barriers can be unhealthy thoughts we have about ourselves or about others. Overcoming, correcting and changing these thoughts is necessary. One example of a person with an intimacy barrier is someone who identifies as a gay man but who believes he is sinful. Another example is an individual who has been abused. These individuals must address the internal story before healthy intimacy is possible. In both cases, online behaviors might be easier due to the reduced fear of getting hurt. Long-term growth will need to address the fear.

External barriers are outside of us. Examples of these barriers may be isolation or a lack of resources to connect with others. Some of the "-isms" such as sexism, racism, and heterosexism are barriers. With these situations, setting up plans to help you address how the external barriers impact your life can be a helpful approach. Other times the barrier may be a lack of skills that negatively influences a person's ability to communicate with others. In these cases, therapy and coaching may be helpful. You will not find intimacy when you shut down and isolate yourself out of fear. Resorting to the Internet – instead of direct, human contact – is one way people have figuratively shut down. Intimacy is learned through trial and error. Intimacy sometimes requires the pain of rejection, failure or betrayal. It is not possible to avoid these risks and have intimacy. Your reaction to life's hurts and fears can lead to opportunities for intimacy. The reality is that the other person is probably just as fearful as you are. The question is, which person will be the first to transcend that fear.

Assignment

- As you review your sexual history and your timeline, describe how intimacy (or the lack of intimacy) and online sexual behavior relate in your experience.

- What are the messages you have heard about touch from your family, culture, religious tradition or community. How well can you ask others to help with meeting your touch intimacy needs?

- Identify the top three types of intimacy most important to you.

- How would you know if these intimacy needs are satisfied in your life?

- Identify 3–5 people who can help you meet those intimacy needs.

- If you are not satisfied with the type of intimacies, or your level of satisfaction, identify a plan to increase your level of satisfaction.

Dating and Sexual Health

As people start addressing their sexual health issues, eventually they start meeting others, including dating and eventually courtship. Below are eight ideas designed to help frame the desire to date as progress, and a tool for your ongoing recovery. Perfection isn't required (or possible), but addressing these concerns will increase your chances for positive experiences.

1. Clarify whether you're ready to date. Dating requires that you have a sense of self, and that you are comfortable in your overall progress. Dating requires assertive communication. It requires that you've defined your basic boundaries including level of disclosure, when disclosure will occur, and a multitude of desires and wants. Examining past dating experiences and addressing triggers that led to relapses is important. One part of this process consists of asking yourself how much you are willing to share about your online behaviors. Talking with your support network and addressing their feedback is also important.

2. Clarify your boundaries about which online and face-to-face behaviors would be acceptable. Set up explicit boundaries about the type of sexual behavior that can or cannot occur. This needs to be clarified before you start dating.

3. Identify your goals. Be honest with yourself and your support network about what you are looking for in your desire to start dating. Are you looking for friendship? Sex? Relationship? Children? None of these goals is better than any of the others, but be honest. Develop the skills to effectively communicate these goals with your potential partners. Communicate and get feedback from your support network.

4. Clarify the types of "date" you want. Sometimes starting small is a better plan. You might go on a "coffee date" on a Saturday morning. You might do a lunch date. Instead of calling it a date, describe it as a social chat or a meet-and-greet. Taking the word "date" off the table, and focusing on the social interaction can reduce stress and anxiety. Scheduling it during the day, or mornings (versus Friday evening) can create clarity regarding your goals.

5. Identify activities that you want to do. In identifying your activities, use it to start conversations about what your potential dating partner likes to do. Think outside the box. Review the suggestions on intimacy to consider alternatives to the classic date. You might go to church, go to a museum, go to lecture, etc.

6. Create safety plans. Before you go, make sure you schedule an escape plan, an "out." If you're going for a coffee date, set up an out at 1 p.m. by saying that you have a meeting with a friend at 1 p.m. And set up a meeting with a person from your support network for 1 p.m. to talk about the experience. If the encounter went well, you can always have a second encounter.

7. Remember dating for what dating is. It's a chance to meet and interact with others. You're not making a lifetime commitment to the person on a single date. By addressing the expectations and assumptions you bring to the conversation, you can maintain your focus.

8. Address known concerns beforehand. For example, if you're an introvert develop topics you feel comfortable sharing and asking about. Make sure you are asking questions versus letting the other person set the agenda. If you're the classic extrovert, make sure you listen as well.

For individuals in an existing relationship damaged by online behavior, it might be helpful to "date" (symbolically) your current partner. Using these ideas may help re-kindle and heal your current relationship.

The Language of Relationships

Much of couples therapy focuses on communication skills. Using the helpful metaphor of language, "undoing the assumption that we all speak the same language" is often the first place of intervention. Consider the following examples. English is the predominant language in the United States, and the assumption is that we all speak English. Yet, even within the United States, in parts of the U.S., different words are used to describe the same concept. For example, New Yorkers enjoying a cola drink might be drinking soda, but Midwesterners enjoying the same drink would be drinking pop. The same holds true in other English speaking countries, like England. Americans on a road trip store their luggage in the trunk of their car, but the English store it in the boot. And when the Americans arrive at their destination, they might take the elevator up to their desired floor, but the English might take the lift. Likewise, there are significant differences between Spanish in Latin America and Spanish in Spain. Even Arabic has multiple dialects, and these differences are barriers to communication. So even though people may speak one common language, it is crucial to be aware of differences present in that one common language. Here, we refer to those differences as "dialects." It is important to learn how to understand and translate those dialects.

Similarly, in relationships, it is important to remember that we all have different dialects of communication. These dialects are informed and shaped by the multiple cultures we belong to (age, race/ethnicity, religion, gender, etc.), our family of origin, and our life history. Often, there is enough commonality to be able to communicate with a partner. Most relationship problems stem from communication problems that show up in the guise of unmet expectations and assumptions, hidden wants and needs, past hurts and pains, and hoped for joys and goals.

A classic example is fighting. In some families, conflict is forbidden. A partner learns that anger cannot be expressed. Another partner may come from a family where conflict is resolved quickly and respectfully. When two partners come together, the dialect of conflict is an obstacle to be resolved. The resolution is often as simple as teaching each other their respective dialects. The same idea can be applied to mundane things, like the level of cleanliness in the house, or difficult areas, such as sexual expression, needs and values.

The difficulty in this process is that much of our dialect regarding relationships is automatic and habitual. We assume everyone has the same language, mannerisms, assumptions, and expectations in a relationship. That assumption is often the source of the relationship problems. Teaching each other your individual dialects, and learning to translate your partner's dialect is a necessary skill for building powerful and strong relationships.

Relationship Satisfaction

Relationship satisfaction is a major component of sexual health. Examine how your online sexual behavior is related to relationship satisfaction. As in other topics, online behavior can be both a cause, and consequence, of relationship satisfaction concerns. In this topic you are encouraged to focus on your level of satisfaction in your current (or most recent) relationship. Long-term personal happiness, health and wellness are correlated with healthy relationships. One of the more difficult tasks in any relationship is being able to talk with your partner(s) comfortably about sex. The issues can range from simply how often to have sex and or what to do during sex, to whether the relationship should be open, monogamous or some variation thereof.

Respond the following statements:

- Talking about sex with my sexual partner(s) is a satisfying experience.   YES / NO
- Overall, I feel satisfied about my current sexual relationship(s).   YES / NO
- I have difficulty finding a sexual partner.   YES / NO
- I feel my sexual partner(s) avoids talking about sexuality with me.   YES / NO
- When I have sex with my sexual partner, I feel emotionally close to him or her.   YES / NO
- Overall, I feel close with my sexual partner(s).   YES / NO
- I have difficulty keeping a sexual partner.   YES / NO

- I feel I can express what I like and don't like sexually.   YES / NO
- I feel my sexual partner(s) is sensitive to my needs and desires.   YES / NO
- Some sexual matters are too upsetting to discuss with my partner(s).   YES / NO

A "yes" response to statements 3 4, 7 and 10 require long-term follow-up. A "no" response to statements 1, 2, 5, 6, 8, 9 require long-term follow-up. Pay attention to the responses that require long-term follow-up. Why did you answer the question the way you did? What are your plans to address the issues raised?

Healing from Past Relationships

When a dog bites a child, there is a high probability that the child will have a negative reaction to dogs in the future. This is an example of transference (see page 47). Any reaction you have to a person is built on your history of experiences. When you have a reaction to a current partner, this reaction is built on your past experiences. When positive, this is helpful. When negative, this can create a barrier that may possibly doom the new relationship.

The amount of hurt arising from past relationships is a major barrier to future relationships. The amount of hurt caused by online sexual behavior affirms the need for healing as well. Before you can begin again, you need to clear away the "garbage" of hurt and anger arising from past relationships. Many people will say they are "over" their ex, or over the partner's online behavior, but our experience suggests otherwise. Review your sexual timeline. How have your past relationships impacted your online sexual behavior and, vice-versa, how has your online sexual behavior impacted your relationships? It is important to have a clear understanding about the connection between your life history and your sexual behavior. Consider the following questions:

- Was your online behavior a response to something your partner did? If so, describe the details?

- Was your partner's behavior in response to something you did? If so, describe the details?

- If applicable, what relationship payoffs were you trying to obtain by engaging in online sexual behavior?

It is important to seek help if there are other issues connected to a past relationship. Sometimes the feelings of grief and hurt are so strong, that some type of grief therapy might be important (see page 122). Other issues to consider as possible barriers to future relationships include depression (see page 108), types and impact of abuse (see page 115), stages of identity development (see page 90) or feelings of shame and guilt (see page 84). Until these are addressed, you may be stuck on an escalator trying to go the wrong way.

Forgiveness in Relationships

Forgiveness is not about forgetting. Forgiveness is not about letting the other person off the hook. Forgiveness is about *your* healing. It includes helping you heal from negative thoughts and at the same time helping you let go of painful feelings. It is also an extreme act of compassion when you can forgive the person who hurt you. In some religious traditions, raising forgiveness to a radical expression is offering compassion to the one who offended you. This brings about YOUR radical transformation.

Here are a number of strategies we have found that are helpful in healing from past relationships. They are designed to help create forgiveness in your life.

- Write a goodbye letter. Share with your support network. Set the letter aside and repeat writing a letter and share again. Repeat again. Keep and review each version. After you've done this 10 times, sit down and review each letter.

You will be able to identify a number of themes. And hopefully, you will be able to see your progress in the healing process. Once you have done this about 10 times, if you choose, you may send the 10th version of the letter.

- Get Support. Reach out to friends, family and professionals.
- Complete an inventory. Honestly assess your role in the relationship conflict. Step out of the victim role. Recognize that "it takes two to tango." Move forward.
- Establish a boundary. Despite what your ex might say, your ex's behavior is about your ex, not you. This is important. Remind yourself of it.

Steps in Building the Sexual Relationship

The main goal in any couple's relationship is open and honest communication between partners about what they want, what they don't want and what makes them happy. When your behaviors match your values, it is a sign of sexual health. It is your responsibility to communicate your values to your partner. The degree to which any behavior is consistent with your values is a decision that ultimately rests with you. Regarding sexual expression with your partner, four general tasks are important:

Tell your partner

Have you told your partner what you like and do not like? Too many times, we have run into couples that say to one another, "I didn't know that." For any number of reasons (shame, low self-esteem, fear of being judged, not wanting to upset their partner), clients will not talk about their likes and dislikes. In many cases, online behaviors may be a result of not knowing how to talk to your partner about what you like or don't like

Ask your partner

Once you know what you like, you should concentrate on what your partner likes and dislikes. It is important not only to know your partners' likes and dislikes but why he or she has these interests. For example, a couple didn't engage in penetration because it physically hurt. It turned out the pain was due to warts, and once that condition was addressed the problem went away.

Learn

Do not be shy if you do not know how to do something. Some online behaviors are attempts to cope with not knowing how to do something. You need to learn some basics regarding foreplay, stimulating the clitoris, stretching the vaginal and or sphincter muscle, proper cleanup and so on. You may need to educate your partner.

Get help

If after going through the first three steps you find you are still having problems, you may want to seek some outside help. This does not necessarily mean therapy or counseling, although professional help is a good option for more challenging problems. Try having a frank "out of the box" conversation in which you look at creative outlets and avenues to get your sexual needs met. These could include talking to your spiritual adviser, attending a sexuality workshop or reading various "how to" books. You might go online together to review possible interventions to address the problems. Each of these interventions might be helpful in breaking the logjam in your relationship.

If you have shared your likes and dislikes with your partner and are still having problems, the next steps requires a bit of hard work and honest discussions between you and your partner.

Prioritizing

Some relationships do not focus on sex because they are rich in other ways, such as shared values or emotional connections (see the section on Intimacy, page 158). Consider the importance of your sexual request. Are you willing to live without it? In looking at the whole picture, you might have to agree not to engage in the behavior. This is often the case in "kinkier" types of sexual behavior. In these cases, online sexual behavior might be one way to get these needs met. If you absolutely are unwilling to live without the type of sexual behavior, consider the next two ideas.

Substituting

If your need or desire is important enough that you choose not to live without it, you and your partner need to negotiate an alternative way to get your sexual needs met. This can be difficult, eliciting significant fear, jealousy and raise other issues. It may require changing the type of your relationship (see below).

Transitioning

In our experience, ongoing and significant problems regarding sex can be symptoms of underlying problems within the relationship. While no one likes to hear it, the failure to arrive at a solution might suggest the relationship may not be a healthy one. An example of behavior in an unhealthy relationship might include saying things like "Yes I'll do it" but never intending to follow through. Constantly trying to persuade your partner to engage in a behavior is manipulation and not a healthy sign. A hard and honest look at your relationship may reveal that it is not healthy and that it may need to end. If you are both stuck in this area and don't see a solution, seeking outside professional help may be the best, and possibly the last, option for you.

Types of Relationships

Culture is very powerful in shaping our view of what is a healthy relationship (see topic on Culture and Stereotypes on page 77). Our current culture emphasizes that sexual behavior should occur within a monogamous relationship, and that only monogamous relationships are healthy. How much do you agree with this expectation? In fact, there are a multitude of different types of relationships. Sexual health requires that you clarify the type of relationship you want. This is a controversial area, and clinicians legitimately differ in their opinions. The primary approach taken in this book is that you have the responsibility to choose the type of life you want to live regarding sexual expression. We mention three types of sexual relationships:

Celibacy and Singledom

Celibacy is often confused with singledom, but it is different. Definitions vary, but we define celibacy as a choice not to engage in any sexual contact with anyone. There are opinions saying that any sexual expression including masturbation, fantasy and use of sexually explicit material go against the idea of celibacy. Other opinions say that celibacy does not allow any genital contact with a person. Some religious traditions impose celibacy as the only form of sexual expression for groups of people (usually LGBT individuals or non-married straight couples). Also, some religious traditions impose celibacy as a discipline in order for a person to qualify to be a minister in that tradition.

Rightfully understood, however, celibacy is less about telling yourself "you can't do that" than about emphasizing something greater in a person's life. Celibacy allows a greater commitment to the major focus in a person's life. In this approach, celibacy is believed to facilitate other types of intimate relationships (see Types of Intimacy on page 158). In our opinion, a healthy expression of celibacy is possible. It does take work and self-understanding. And celibacy doesn't "turn-off" the sexual energy within a person. If you choose this, you *must* find *healthy* ways to channel your sexual energy. It is very important to choose celibacy for the right reason. We've run into many individuals who "choose" celibacy out of fear, a history of abuse, or low self-esteem. If these are the motivating factors for choosing celibacy, it is only a matter of time until a commitment or vow of celibacy will be broken.

Singledom is the choice to remain single and not be in a relationship. Often, people do not consider singledom as a choice, given the assumption from the primary culture that everyone should be in a relationship. The pressure toward coupling is profound and subtle. Watch what happens with your couple-friends when you break up a relationship. Think about Grandma's first comment when you go home for the holidays: "Have you found someone yet?" It is an expression of concern for your happiness, but it does demonstrate the social pressure toward coupling, and it implies that something is wrong with remaining single. Singledom is simply an option on how to live out your life. It may, or may not, include celibacy. It may be short or long term. It is simply a choice. As in all other choices, the reason that you are choosing to be single is the key question for you. Understanding your motivations (including perhaps some of the unspoken reasons) is a key to sexual health.

Monogamy

Most of this book is built on an assumption of monogamy. Monogamy is typically defined as sexual contact exclusively between two individuals within some type of committed relationship. Even this definition has different interpretations, resulting in confusion and conflict. For some people, monogamy is expanded to prevent any emotional relationships with anyone but the primary partner. Some interpretations of monogamy also view use of sexually explicit material as a violation of monogamy. So, for some couples, online sexual behavior would be a violation of the commitment to monogamy, but in other couples, this would be okay. The key is for you and your partner to clarify your opinions.

Healthy monogamy is about trust and commitment. It means working with your partner to put the other first. And – paradoxically – in putting the other first, your needs are met, in part because your partner is putting you first. Monogamy isn't passive – it requires tremendous amounts of work. This book is designed to start the necessary conversations regarding healthy monogamy, to make it possible for you to choose monogamy for the right reasons. When monogamy is chosen out of fear, it is less about an expression of love than an expression of fear and attempted control over your partner. There is a decided lack of trust. (The same concerns exist in choosing celibacy or singledom. Celibacy or singledom chosen out of fear probably are not healthy choices.)

Open/Poly Relationships

Open relationships are typically defined as a relationship where there exists a primary sexual and emotional partner followed by a secondary partner or partners. (Given the focus of the book, there isn't the space to fully address poly relationships and alternative relationships. For more information, read *Ethical Slut* by Easton and Litsz or check out www.xeromag.com.) Within the concept of Open/Poly relationships, there are a variety of definitions and expressions. If you choose an open relationship it is important for you and your primary partner to clarify ground rules and expectations. When, where, with whom and how often are all topics to be addressed. What are the plans for communicating and coping with fear, jealousy and insecurity? What are the safer-sex rules?

If you want an open relationship, examine what unmet needs (if any) exist within your primary relationship. Significant reflection should occur within your support network to clarify the reasons you want an open relationship. In particular, be careful that you are not simply trying to get out of the primary relationship. If the primary relationship is not healthy, it is important to address the issues first. If it should end, do this with integrity instead of forcing a rift that ends the relationship. One guideline is that all partners be open and honest in the conversation. Both partners must agree with a sense of internal integrity with any decision. It might be better to end a relationship than agree to a type of relationship that is inconsistent with your values.

Sexual satisfaction is a major component of overall relationship satisfaction. Research has repeatedly stressed that overall health is connected to relationship satisfaction. If you continue to struggle in this area, we strongly recommend seeking additional help from a qualified professional.

Assignment

- Review your sexual timeline, online sexual behavior and relationship history for any patterns. Consider if your behavior was in response to something your partner did? Was your partner's behavior in response to something you did? If so, describe the details.

- If applicable, what relationship payoffs where you trying to obtain by engaging in online sexual behavior?

- If applicable, what steps do you need to take for continued healing in your relationships?

- Clarify what type of relationship you want in your life. Explain this to your support network. Review this with your partner.

- Identify plans to address the concerns raised by each of these questions.

Finding a Relationship Therapist

As couples recover from the consequences of Internet sexual behavior, the healing sometimes needs outside support and feedback. Finding a couple's therapist, or a relationship therapist, is important, but it can be difficult. Ask your support network and current therapist for suggestions. Not every therapist has training in relationship therapy. Review the following questions and suggestions to help you in the process.

Before you start, to the best of your ability clarify your goal. While it might be hard to acknowledge, if you know that you don't want to stay in the relationship, be honest up front for the sanity of everyone. This includes your sanity, your partner's sanity and the clinician's sanity.

Many times the individuals in the relationship will start therapy during a rocky period. If either one of the individuals is unsure about the future of the relationship, your therapist may ask for a time commitment from both of you to discern your intentions and to work on the relationship.

Remember that the RELATIONSHIP is the client, not the individuals. Most individual therapists will NOT do relationship therapy when working with one member of the relationship. There are appropriate exceptions, so this is not an absolute rule. Check with the therapist.

During the intake session, put everything on the table, whether it is sexual issues, insecurity, jealousy, communication, respect, or whatever. Often, the second and third sessions are individual meetings to provide each individual an opportunity to put additional issues on the table that may be too difficult in the first session. Sharing everything is important. For example, if you engage in alternative sexual behaviors, or if you had a sexual contact outside the relationship, say so.

A juggling metaphor in relationship therapy helps to demonstrate the challenge of relationship therapy. At the start of relationship therapy, there are three balls to juggle: Person A, Person B, and the Relationship. The "three balls" of relationship therapy make creating change in the relationship more difficult than individual therapy. It is important for both individuals to have realistic expectations about the timing of disclosure in light of overall progress.

Disclosure to Partners

We recommend sharing the following few pages with your partner sooner than later. This was referenced in the introduction on page 12.

When people address their online sexually compulsive behavior, it affects their partners as well. For the partner, a variety of issues must be addressed, including emotional, physical and sexual issues. We recommend that the partner obtain therapy or support as well. Through individual therapy, we recommend that both partners clarify their respective commitments to the future of the relationship before disclosing online sexually compulsive behavior. A partner's disclosure of online sexually compulsive behavior triggers a parallel, coping process for the other partner. Treatment includes getting information, including "understanding" the language of people in the field. Therapists and those involved in the 12-step movement often use a jargon for shorthand communication. Learning the meaning of these terms is important. As you move away from crisis and shock, stay focused on your emotional and physical health. Incidentally, if the computer is shared, family members may have access to sexually explicit material – it is nearly impossible to fully remove all inappropriate files. It becomes important to address basic safety issues and to set boundaries to maintain other people's safety.

As a person copes with a partner's online compulsive behavior, it is important for the person to triage priorities. The person must identify what has to be done today, in the next month, the next three months and the next year. Partners typically have feelings of despair, hopelessness, confusion, and anger. Shock, depression and grief may also occur. Sometimes individuals blame themselves, either due to ignoring signs or simply not knowing. Part of the healing process is to gain support from professionals, peer networks (groups) and family or spiritual support.

If the online behavior moved beyond virtual encounters and led to an actual encounter, the partner may be at increased risk for HIV/STIs. We recommend that you meet with your health care provider. Be completely open and honest about the purpose of the visit. Some providers will assume that individuals in a relationship, are not at risk for HIV/STI. The individual will need to be explicit and say, "I found out my partner has multiple sex partners and I'm worried about being infected with a sexually transmitted infection." The partnership will need to determine safer-sex guidelines in light of any risky behaviors.

After both individuals have addressed their respective issues, couples therapy can facilitate the healing of the relationship. Relationship issues can address "blaming" statements by the partner. Often there is a sense of powerlessness that comes with not knowing what to do and how to get your partner to stop the behaviors. Treatment for the individual and the partner includes clarifying what you both need and want in a relationship and assessing honestly where the current relationship is going. This is a chance for you to clarify your boundaries and develop the skills to protect those boundaries. Some partners may feel pressured by their support network to leave the relationship. Unfortunately, no guidelines are available for the decisions you and your partner might need to make. Some relationships can continue; others should end. If you know you are not going to stay in the relationship, disclosure of your online sexually compulsive behavior is not necessary. If you know you want to stay in the relationship, such disclosure can occur. We will not work with couples that use the process of disclosure as ammunition against each other. In this approach, disclosure is about repairing, reconciling and taking full responsibility in order to foster an ongoing relationship.

What do you share?

After discovering that his partner was engaging in online sexual behavior that violated their relationship rules, a client commented that coping with identity theft was easier than coping with the loss of his image of the relationship. He reported that he felt like a part of his identity was ripped away. The metaphor is accurate.

Disclosure is the process of sharing parts of your treatment history, sexual history, sexual behaviors and timeline. Disclosure may include all of these aspects, or only parts of material.

One of the biggest issues in addressing sexual health is the question of whether a partner should disclose to the other partner, sexual behavior that violates the relationship rules Not everyone agrees, but our bias is toward full disclosure or at least giving the partner the right to set the level of disclosure. Your treatment process, as set forth in this section, is designed to help you respond to your partner's needs.

One issue rarely addressed is the disclosure of your history to any future partners. The timing and level of detail of your future disclosures are important to consider.

You wouldn't necessarily avoid disclosure of a chemical addiction or health issue, and we see the issue of sexual history as similar. We also recommend working with a couple's therapist to help you and your partner through the process.

Assignment

These following questions are for your partner to answer before you start any disclosure process. Review your partner's responses before your disclosure.

- Who is your primary support network? What is your plan to reach out for support when your partner completes his or her disclosure?

- What therapy of overall person growth work have you done to address treatment issues triggered by your partner's online or offline sexual behavior?

- What are your feelings and thoughts about disclosure?

- Are you committed to staying in the relationship? If not, we do not recommend disclosure. If you are ambivalent, why do you want disclosure at this time? What work do you need to complete in order to strengthen your commitment to the relationship before disclosure?

- What is your goal of disclosure?

- How much detail do you want to receive? Consider the following:

  - Your partner completed a sex history and timeline? The sex history (see page 27) is very detailed (about 4 pages) and includes questions addressing frequency, intensity, consequences (legal, medical, financial), duration, location, types of behaviors, number of partners, online behaviors, etc. Which of these questions would you like answered?

  - Your partner completed a timeline (see page 34). Would you like to see this timeline? At what time in your partner's history do you want him to start (Since dating? Last disclosure? Lifetime?)

  - Often there are additional acting out behaviors, would you like to know about these compulsive/addictive behaviors?

  - Is there any information you DON'T want disclosed to you?

- Your partner has identified a continuing care plan addressing the major high-risk situations, thinking errors, and feeling triggers related to your partner's online sexual behaviors. Would you like your partner to share this plan?

- Are you prepared to respond to your partner with your own disclosures (if appropriate)? Why or why not?

Assignment

These are questions for the user of this workbook to answer.

- What is your plan regarding addressing your partners request for the type and amount of disclosure?

- What feelings and thoughts do you anticipate in preparing for disclosure?

- What are the barriers toward full disclosure? What are your plans to address these barriers?

Spirituality, Values and Sexual Health

This section addresses spirituality and sexual health. All three of us are supportive of religious traditions. There are some tremendous sexual health values taught by many religious traditions. But we also recognize that too often in sexuality, religious messages may actually be a barrier to sexual health. A distinction between religion and spirituality is offered. A journey toward sexual health may require alternatives to a religious tradition. For many, the concept of a higher power is helpful. Nevertheless, a common theme in both religious and spiritual traditions is recognition of the importance of core values that shape your life. We end this section by identifying strategies that you can use to help in your process of identifying the core values that you use to define your personal definition of sexual health.

In many ways, spirituality can shape and focus our values, goals and behaviors. The goal for this section is to help you clarify how consistent your values are concerning sexual behavior.

It is important to start the conversation about spirituality by introducing a distinction between spirituality and religion. The distinction reflects the difference between the individual and the community. "Spirituality" reflects your faith, values, and experiences of the holy. "Religion" reflects the community's faith, values and experiences of the holy. The two are different but related.

It is through one's experience of spirituality that one connects with a community of faith. To develop one's spirituality, it may be helpful to review your understanding of scripture and tradition to create a positive approach to morality and higher power. Scripture and tradition are not always an enemy to spirituality. Within a tradition, a sense of wholeness and acceptance is possible. Tradition expresses a community's experience of "God" or "The Holy." This is true whether it is a long-term tradition (such as Jewish, Christian, Muslim, Catholic, Buddhist traditions) or a newer tradition (such as fellowship after a 12-step group).

Barriers to Spirituality

Three barriers to spirituality are religiosity, fundamentalism and lack of education. Consider how these barriers may be present in your life.

Religiosity is based on the performance of duties without the integration of spiritual values. Early on, we discussed the need for integrity (see page 9). Many individuals profess a faith but fail to live by that faith. Their behavior is focused on appearances, on looking good, and using religion as a means of looking good. The number of public sex scandals by those who profess a religious tradition proves this point. In emphasizing a healthy life, many religious traditions actually suppress sexuality versus finding healthy outlets. Religiosity is one means of suppressing sexuality.

Fundamentalism occurs in two primary ways: scriptural fundamentalism and dogmatic fundamentalism. Essentially, fundamentalism sets up a thinking error that one view of scripture or belief is the only right view. This creates a series of judgments about who qualifies as a person of faith. Fundamentalism dictates only a narrow manner in which faith can be expressed. In an attempt to help people, the fundamentalist approach usually results in excluding many people.

Lack of education is a final barrier. Many people simply have too little education in their faith tradition to begin the process of uncovering the richness of that tradition. Not many individuals can explain the dogmas and doctrines that can provide a rich resource for future growth.

As you move toward increased spiritual health, it might be helpful to address any struggles you have had with fundamentalism or with feeling judged and rejected. It may also be helpful to increase your education within your tradition. Addressing your struggles and increasing your education might help affirm your sexual health and clarify your values.

Sin is doing something wrong; Hell is staying in something wrong.

As individuals move forward in recovery, we hear stories of relapse. In psychological terms, we might describe an acting-out encounter and make reference to stopping the behavior as we move forward. In 12-step language we might describe this as relapse, and highlight the power needed to stop the addiction. In spiritual language, we might recognize this as sin and the need to seek forgiveness. Each of the different frameworks helps us understand the same behavior through a different lens.

Using the spiritual framework, a personal definition of hell builds on the concept of sin. If sin is doing something wrong, hell is staying in something wrong. After a relapse, individuals enter into shame spirals, emotionally abuse themselves, and forever put themselves in a negative place. For many of these individuals, they punish themselves much more than anyone else could ever punish them. The individuals are in a self-imposed hell distinguished as helplessness, frustration, and hopelessness.

When we meet an individual in this self-imposed hell, we encourage them toward self-forgiveness. A helpful question is, what would happen if the individual would treat others they way they are treating themselves (a reverse Golden Rule)? And we encourage them to "be gentle with yourself." This isn't about letting yourself off the hook, but treating yourself with the level of compassion each individual deserves. Developing sexual health requires accountability that is respectful and that leads toward forgiveness and healing versus shame, fear, and the ongoing experience of a personal hell.

Power of Story

The process of developing spirituality is to recognize the importance of "story." Spirituality starts and ends with a theology of story. This is a process where we identify experiences of God. (For convenience, we use the term, "God," but included are such terms as, "Higher Power," "Goddess," "Spirit," "Wisdom," "The Absolute," "The "All," etc.) A theology of story helps us recognize that scripture is simply a collection of stories of people's experiences of God. Typically, these oral stories were written down, collected and made official across time. In other words, a person had an experience of God, and then shared the experience with another person who was also so inspired that he shared it with others. People wrote down and collected these stories. This collection eventually became what we see as "scripture."

The application of a theology of story to our daily life is important. A theology of story asks, "What experiences of God in my life have I encountered?" It is in recognizing these experiences that we begin the process of seeing how God is present in our life. The difficulty is that we have lost the ability to share new stories. Many people deny their experiences of the holy. Furthermore, because of fundamentalism, scriptures have unfortunately become a basis to condemn people instead of being a collection of people's experience of God. The use of scriptures as a weapon has led to a difficulty of sharing our personal stories.

Part of the process of developing your spirituality is to understand how we experience God in various ways by discussing three approaches to developing spirituality: **positive spirituality, generativity** and **creative mythology**. Each can give you insight into your own story of God experiences. **Positive spirituality** emphasizes a process of uncovering the values by which you choose to live your life. It is future oriented. We make decisions and express our values as a reflection of our experience of God. Positive spirituality focuses on goals or values such as wholeness, integrity, fidelity and growth that a person seeks to express. For those with a religious tradition, the values we choose to live by can come from our community experience. Many values identified in the scriptures and traditions are positive. Examples include love, integrity, forgiveness and responsibility. These values shape our life. A typical example of this is the WWJD ("What Would Jesus Do?") bumper sticker. A person with a WWJD sticker has declared "As a Christian, who believes in Jesus, I use His life to shape my behavior as an expression of my beliefs."

Positive spirituality is future focused, but **generativity** focuses on the now. Generativity asks the question, "How am I being made whole in the now?" In other words, in this experience (or with this thought) "Am I brought to a sense of wholeness, or am I left distracted and broken. In the realm of sexual health, does this behavior help or hinder my well-being?"

The concept of **creative mythology** is based on research by Joseph Campbell. For him, creative mythology focuses on how people express meaning in their lives. He says creative mythology is "present when an individual has an experience of order, horror, beauty, exhilaration, which seeks to be communicated through signs, images, and words."

Campbell's research suggests that a focus on the experience of something amazing, either good or bad, shifts an individual's understanding of reality, and that in these experiences a person connects to God. Then, the person shares his experiences with other people. Creative mythology is an attempt to identify and express meaning of something greater in a person's life by noticing these important experiences. Mythology is a way one person's heart speaks to another person's heart. Notice the similarity between creative mythology and the concept of intimacy, as discussed in the topic Intimacy (see page 158).

(see page 158)

Assignment

This assignment will help you to start thinking about something greater in your life. Think "big" about your future. What would a "life you love" look like? Spirituality requires you to make a commitment to take responsibility in your life. You need to step forward to identify and claim the values that you find important, the values that you will use to shape your life. What works for some people person will not necessarily work for you. We may learn from each other, but our path is uniquely our own.

- Identify three people who inspire you. These people may be real or fictional, living or dead, someone you know, or simply someone you've read about. For each person, identify why this person is an inspiration to you. Examine two or three values this person has expressed through their life. As you think about each person, you may start to identify themes that are important to you.

- Name three times when you experienced a sense of timelessness. Some authors describe this as "being in the flow" (see Power of Thought, page 43). In this context, "timelessness" is the experience of time passing without your awareness. Think of a young child playing outside all day. You say to the child "Come in for bed." To the child, the day passed with a sense of timelessness. They simply were completely in the moment. Describe the settings in which you experienced timelessness, focusing on who, what, when, and where. What words do you use to summarize how these experiences inspire you?

- As you examine the individuals and experiences in your life that are important, make note of common themes, values and experiences. These themes are expressions of your experience of God in your daily life.

- After listing the themes, review each word in a dictionary or Wikipedia. Learn the depth of meaning of these words. Summarize what you learn.

List three to five values that express your spirituality. Below are some examples. These values are broad and primarily evoke a calling to move beyond the big and little fears of life and step into a greater life. In the field of morality, we might label these values as virtues. Find the values that inspire you. Examples of possible values include the following. (If you find one that you like, continue to research the term.)

Justice

Justice is often reduced to holding people accountable, sort of like a punishment. This is a start, but justice is also about restoring a sense of harmony and connection. Justice is more than just fairness; it's also about the common good.

Peace

Peace is the absence of conflict, but it also includes the ideas of harmony, connection and common purpose. Peace also refers to a sense of internal purpose, being grounded and a sense of internal acceptance. Within the concept of peace is a connection to justice.

Generosity

Generosity is often seen as giving to others on a monetary level. Generosity can also include giving of talent and time. Included are the concepts of focusing on others and the common good. Generosity is giving someone the benefit of the doubt by interpreting comments and statements from a view toward growth instead of failure.

Love

Love often focuses on a strong emotional attachment. The English understanding of Love is based on the term "charity," which can include a sense of unconditional acceptance of another person.

Wisdom

Wisdom is more than intelligence; it's the application of experience with knowledge. Within the concept is a sense of integrity and being grounded. Applying wisdom creates justice. Wisdom can also include leading by experience.

Compassion

Compassion is about caring for others. It includes the profound understanding of another's experience. It's about entering into a conversation with a willingness to understand another person's point of view, even if you disagree. Compassion calls forth justice and wisdom.

Courage

Courage includes the concept of bravery. It's not just about acting without fear; it's also about acting through fear. You will experience fear moving forward; courage is about continuing to move forward. Sharing everything with your support network is an example of courage. Courage primarily occurs when you face a struggle or challenge.

Integrity

Integrity requires a level of self-awareness and commitment to live according to the inner truth. This means saying what you mean, and meaning what you say. Honoring your word is a major part of integrity. Integrity occurs when your behaviors and values are consistent with one another.

Your Values

Your task is to identify values that are important to you. Ask yourself how your values shape your behaviors, your limits, your response to fears and your boundaries. Does a particular sexual behavior move you closer or further away from your values? Our experience suggests that when we are living lives based on our values, we are living lives we love.

The challenge is to ask yourself, "How willing am I to do whatever it takes to express my values in living?" Our inspirations are often people who, despite their fear, choose actions that express their values. Think of people such as Martin Luther King Jr., Gandhi and Mother Theresa. They expressed their values in their daily lives to the degree that the world recognized them as inspiring.

The values that inspire you are remarkably stable, yet they can sometimes change. More often it is our awareness, language and skill in understanding and expressing our values that change, more than our values themselves. Please pay attention to both the typical meaning as well as the philosophical meaning of the values that are most important to you. Forgiveness, for example, has many layers of meaning. Value clarification is a continuing process. It is a process, not a product. You can use your values to shape your continuing-care plan in a profound way. The key questions are, "Will this behavior protect my values?" and "How do my values shape the next step for me?"

Using the values listed above – justice, peace, generosity, wisdom, compassion, courage and integrity – simply as starting points with the addition of any other values you identified, the five values that are most important to me are:

1.

2.

3.

4.

5.

Stage 3: Setting the Next Step

We believe that personal growth never really ends. We do believe, however, that the need for formal therapy can end. In preparation for the next steps, this stage is about consolidating the lessons learned in Stages 1 and 2 by summarizing the primary issues and current plans to address the issues. Your final assignment will be to complete an Internet health plan where you define healthy and unhealthy online behaviors.

Continuing Care Plan

The story of a "canary in a coal mine" is a classic story of how, before the development of modern equipment, miners would take a caged canary with them when they went into the mine. They used the canary as a warning sign to let them know the level of unsafe gases. Because of their size and susceptibility, canaries reacted to these gases more quickly than humans. If the miners saw the canary was ill, sick or dead, they would evacuate the mine for their safety. Similarly, knowing your early warning signs (in the form of feeling triggers, thinking errors and high risks), you can follow through with plans for prevention and safety.

Assignment

This assignment focuses on preventing the acting-out cycle by identifying plans for the most important factors in your acting-out cycle. You can obtain these items by reviewing your previous work. List five of each of the following: thinking errors (see page 48), feeling triggers (see page 57) and high-risk situations (see page 60).

In Stage 1 you started identifying examples of the acting-out cycle. Pay particular attention to your sex history (see page 24), and sex timeline (see page 27). Review any behavior analyses that you completed (see page 72) and your Internet activity log (see page 40). You can also review the topic areas in Stage 2 (see page 73) related to your acting-out cycle (see page 42) and your Internet timeline (see page 34). Notice that you have done most of this work already. This assignment is about bringing together all of the pieces of the puzzle so that you can see the picture in the puzzle.

Next, identify three plans to each item identified. We use the term "SMART" plans. SMART plans have the following characteristics.

- Specific: The plans are detailed and explicit.
- Measurable: You can determine if the plan has been followed. We usually have a number associated with this. (1 person, 1 phone call, 1 date, 1 time, 1 hr., etc.).
- Attainable: It is something you can complete in the established time.
- Relevant: The plan is connected to the triggers, feeling or high-risk situation.
- Timely: You will have the goal completed within a set time frame.

An example is depression as a feeling trigger. Using the SMART framework, you can develop plans to cope. Three smart plans include:

- Take my medications as prescribed.

- Continue to meet once every two weeks with my therapist.

- Talk to one member of my support network daily.

Each of the tasks identified for depression is a SMART plan reflecting the definition of SMART. As a support person, someone would be able to ask, "Did you call?" "Did you take your meds?" and so forth. These plans are difficult to create, but once created they become helpful in addressing barriers to overall health. This is important. When stuck in the depth of the trigger, a pre-established SMART plan is a recipe for getting out of the bad situation.

High-Risk Situations

1. _____

Plans for coping:

-

-

-

2. _____

Plans for coping:

-

-

-

3. _____

Plans for coping:

-

-

-

4. _____

Plans for coping:

-

-

-

5. _____

Plans for coping:

-

-

-

Thinking Errors

1. _____

Plans for coping:

-

-

-

2. _____

Plans for coping:

-

-

-

3. _____

Plans for coping:

-

-

-

4. _____

Plans for coping:

-

-

-

5. _____

Plans for coping:

-

-

-

Feeling Triggers

1. _____

Plans for coping:

-

-

-

2. _____

Plans for coping:

-

-

-

3. _____

Plans for coping:

-

-

-

4. _____

Plans for coping:

-

-

-

5. _____

Plans for coping:

-

-

-

Your plan for sexual health in an electronic world

Our final assignment is also about integration. Given the continuing care plan, it is also important to assess the specific Internet behaviors that contribute to acting out situations, or that otherwise cross personal boundaries. There are many variations of the following assignment. One way is to create three circles where you address the following:

Outer Circle Are Acceptable Behaviors

These behaviors are any Internet behaviors that are healthy in your world. The difficulty is that many individuals want us to tell them the answers to this question, but the key is that you have to define these. Others might provide feedback and suggestions, but in the end you MUST clarify and determine what are acceptable behaviors in YOUR world. What are you willing to commit?

Middle Circle Are Cautious Behaviors

These behaviors often have a "depends" linked to them. Sometimes the same behavior at work is acceptable, but at home is unacceptable (or vice versa).

Anything you can't clarify as healthy/unhealthy, needs to go here. You might be able to use the "depends" to gain further insight into risk factors in your life. As appropriate, clarify the "depends" component of these behaviors as much as possible. One example was a client who could surf the Internet at home until 9 p.m.. At 9 p.m., he started to get tired and moved into the trance often associated with compulsive online behaviors. Surfing the Internet until 9 was a cautious behavior, because he had to make sure his plans were in place to prevent surfing after 9 p.m.

Inner Circles are Unacceptable Behaviors.

These are behaviors that you have determined are unhealthy in any and all cases. For some people, any explicit sexual online behavior at work is unhealthy. Surfing for porn or engaging in sexual chat conversations may fit here. Certain types of websites might fit here. The key is that YOU must agree to any behaviors that are defined as unacceptable.

Assignment:

Behaviors to consider include the following. It is also important to link these behaviors to any qualifiers. This is a start, and isn't an exhaustive list. Examine your history to address additional behaviors not listed here.

- What devices can you use to access the Internet (e.g. computers, smart phones, iPads, etc.)?
- How frequently can you use the Internet?
- Where can you access the Internet (e.g. work, home, friends, relatives)?
- Who should be or needs to be around you, as appropriate?
- What types of websites are acceptable? Think typical web sites such as banks, but also a typical hookup site?
- What types of online sexual activity can be explored (e.g., fetishes such as certain ethnicities, feet, diapers…)?
- Identify if engaging in sexually charged chat, online relationships, virtual sex, exhibitionism or voyeurism online is acceptable
- What email accounts can you use?
- Is it acceptable to use the Internet to arrange real-time hook-ups?
- Is posting online erotic or sexual pictures/videos of yourself or others (including via webcam) acceptable?
- Is it acceptable to masturbate to online sexual materials or activities? Explain why or why not.
- Can you fantasize to online sexual materials or activities? Explain why or why not.
- What sex toys that connect to your computer are acceptable?
- What other sexual activities have you engaged in while online that would be important to review?
- What do you share with your support network?
- What do you share with your partner?

Review and Repeat

Now that you have finished the workbook, it's only appropriate to start again. We see this as a continuing process. An expert is someone with a depth of knowledge, and our goal is to help you become an expert in YOUR life. We recommend you update and review your continuing care plan and your Internet sexual health plan every three months. We also recommend that you go through your responses to the workbook assignments at least yearly. Our experience is that clients have new levels of understanding when they review past assignments. Pay attention to the sex history and the weekly sexual behavior log. Ongoing analyses of these assignments may provide insight into creating a new breakthrough. Repeating assignments may allow new understanding of previously forgotten materials or new understanding of your relationships. A decrease in feelings of shame may allow you to finally deal with a deeper secret not previously shared.

Thank You

We end with an expression of gratitude. You made it! And we're happy to have been part of the process. While we weren't there in your particular journey, you join a virtual community of individuals developing sexual health online and offline. This is a work of passion for us, and our goal in this workbook and other venues is transformation in people's lives.

Additional Resources

We keep an updated bibliography at: www.Internetbehavior.com/cybersexunplugged

Adams, Kenneth (1991) *Silently Seduced: Understanding Covert Incest*, Deerfield Beach: Health Communications.

Amen, Daniel (1998*) Change Your Brain, Change Your Life*, New York: Times Books, 1998.

Are you a workaholic? (2008) http://www.hinduonnet.com/jobs/0011/05080033.htm

Black, Claudia (1982) *It Will Never Happen to Me*, Denver: M.A.C. Publications.

Bradshaw, John (1998) *Healing the Shame That Binds You*, Deerfield Beach, FL: Health Communications.

Bradshaw, John (1990) *Homecoming*, New York: Bantam Books.

Burns D (1980) *Feeling Good: The New Mood Therapy*, New York: Avon Books

Coleman, E. (1991). Compulsive sexual behavior: New concepts and treatments. *Journal of Psychology and Human Sexuality, 4*(2), 37-52.

Coleman, E. (1992). Is your patient suffering from compulsive sexual behavior. *Psychiatric Annals, 22*(6), 320-325.

Coleman, E., Raymond, N., & McBean, A. (2003). Assessment and treatment of compulsive sexual behavior. *Minnesota Medicine, 86*(7), 42-47.

Coleman, E. (1995). Treatment of compulsive sexual behavior. In R. Rosen, & S. R. Leiblum (Eds.), *Case studies in sex therapy* (pp. 333-349). New York, NY: Guilford Press.

Cooper, A., Griffin-Shelley E. (2002) A Quick Tour of Online Sexuality Part. *Annals of the American Psychotherapy Association*, 5

Corley D & Schneider (2002) Disclosing Secrets: When, to Whom and How Much to Reveal Gentle Path Press.

Co-Sex Addicts Anonymous (COSA) http://www.cosa-recovery.org/

Cotton, M. Ball, C., & Robinson, P. (2003) Four Simple Questions Can Help Screen for Eating Disorders *Journal General Internal Medicine*, 18(1): *53–56*.doi: 10.1046/j.1525-1497.2003.20374.x.

Dayton, Tian (2000) *Trauma and Addiction*, Deerfield Beach, FL: Health Communications.

Dube SR et al. (2005) Long-term consequences of childhood sexual abuse by gender of victim. *American Journal of Preventive Medicine* 28(5).

Edwards. E (1993) Development of a New Scale for Measuring Compulsive Buying Behavior *Financial Counseling and Planning*, 4, 67-85.

Edwards, W. M., & Coleman E. (2004). Defining sexual health: A descriptive overview. *Archives of Sexual Behavior*, 33(3), 189-195.

Fisher, B., Cullen, F. & Turner M. (2000) The Sexual Victimization of College Women. National Institute of Justice.

Friel, John & Friel, Linda (1988), *Adult Children: The Secrets of Dysfunctional Families*, Deerfield Beach, FL: Health Communications.

Goldhor, Harriet (1985) *The Dance of Anger,* Lerner, New York: Harper.

Goldhor, Harriet (1990) *The Dance of Intimacy*, New York: Harper,

Goldhor, Harriet (2001) *The Dance of Connection*, New York: Harper.

Hemfelt, R. & Warren, P. (1990) *Kids Who Carry Our Pain.* Nashville: Thomas Nelson.

Hunter, Mic. (1991) *Abused Boys: The Neglected Victims of Sexual Abuse*, New York: Fawcett Books, 1991.

Illinois Institute for Addiction Recovery (2008) What behaviors indicate compulsive shopping and spending? http://www.addictionrecov.org/spendwhat.htm

Lew, M. (1990) *Victims No Longer: Men Recovering from Incest and Other Sexual Child Abuse*, New York: Harper & Row.

Love, Patricia (1990) *Emotional Incest Syndrome*, Patricia Love, New York: Bantam Books.

Lesieur, H. & Blume, S. (2008) The South Oaks Gambling Screen (SOGS) located at: http://www.addictionrecov.org/southoak.htm

Mellody, P., Wells-Miller, A., Miller, J. Keith (2003) *Facing Co Dependency*. HarperOne

Mellody, P., Wells-Miller, A., Miller, J. Keith (2003) *Facing Love Addiction*. HarperOne

Meston, C. & Buss, D. (2007) Why Humans Have Sex. *Archives of Sexual Behavior* 36, 477–507. DOI 10.1007/s10508-007-9175-2

Milkman, H. & Suderwirth, S (1987) *Craving for Ecstasy: The Consciousness and Chemistry of Escape*, Lexington, MA: Lexington Press. ISBN 0669152811.

National Institute on Alcohol Abuse and Alcoholism. (1995). *Assessing alcohol problems: A guide for clinicians and researchers* (NIH No. 95-3745). Bethesda, MD:National Institute of Health

Prevalence of Eating Disorders found at: http://www.eatingdisorderscoalition.org/reports/statistics.html

Robinson, B. E., Uhl G., Miner, M., Bockting, W. O., Scheltema, K. E., Rosser, B. R. S., & Westover, B. (2002). Evaluation of a sexual health approach to prevent HIV among low income, urban, primarily African American women: Results of a randomized controlled trial. *AIDS Education and Prevention, 14* (Suppl. A), 81-96.

Rosser, S., Bockting, W., Ross, M., Miner, M. & Coleman, E. (2008) The Relationship Between Homosexuality, Internalized Homo-Negativity, and Mental Health in Men Who Have Sex with Men. *Journal of Homosexuality*, 55:1, 1-29, doi:10.1080/00918360802129394.

Sandford, Linda (1990) *Strong at the Broken Places*, Linda T. Sanford, New York: Avon Books.

Scarce, Michael (2001) *Male on Male Rape: The hidden toll of stigma and shame*. Basic Books

Schneider, Jennifer (2005) *Back From Betrayal*, Third Edition, Chapin

Sex Addicts Recovery Resources http://www.sarr.org/coaddicts/default.htm

Smalley, Gary & Trent J. (1986) *The Blessing*, Nashville, TN: Thomas Nelson,

Smalley, Gary & Trent J. (1993) *The Blessing Workbook*, Nashville: Thomas Nelson.

Whitefield, Charles (1987) *Healing the Child Within*, Deerfield Beach, FL: Health Communications.

Endnotes

---

[1] Robinson, B. E., Uhl G., Miner, M., Bockting, W. O., Scheltema, K. E., Rosser, B. R. S., & Westover, B. (2002). Evaluation of a sexual health approach to prevent HIV among low income, urban, primarily African American women: Results of a randomized controlled trial. *AIDS Education and Prevention, 14* (Suppl. A), 81-96.

[2] If you want to read additional resources, please read *Slowing Down to the Speed of Life* by Carlson and Bailey, *Flow: The Psychology of Optimal Experience* by Csikszentmihalyi, and *Blink: The Power of Thinking Without Thinking* by Gladwell, and The *Power of Now* by Tolle.

[3] See Malcom Gladwell, *Blink*

[4] Meston, C. & Buss, D. (2007) Why Humans Have Sex. *Archives of Sexual Behavior* 36, 477–507. DOI 10.1007/s10508-007-9175-2

[5] The Diagnostic and Statistical Manual, 4th Edition, Text Revised published by the American Psychiatric Association is the standard reference text among mental health clinicians. You can review much of this material online.

[6] National Institute on Alcohol Abuse and Alcoholism. (1995). *Assessing alcohol problems: A guide for clinicians and researchers* (NIH No. 95-3745). Bethesda, MD: National Institute of Health

[7] Cotton, M. Ball, C., & Robinson, P (2003) Four Simple Questions Can Help Screen for Eating Disorders *Journal General Internal Medicine*, 18(1): *53–56*.doi: 10.1046/j.1525-1497.2003.20374.x.

[8] Edwards. E. (1993) Development of a New Scale for Measuring Compulsive Buying Behavior Financial Counseling and Planning, 4, 67-85.

[9] Bradshaw, John (1998) Healing the Shame that Binds You. HCI

[10] In a few rare circumstances, the external genitalia may be confusing. For more information, search out the term "intersex" on the Internet.

[11] Adapted from http://www.helpguide.org/mental/suicide_help.htm)

[12] Fisher, Cullen & Turner, 2000

[13] Dube, 2005.

[14] Scarce, 2001.

[15] Adapted from Body Love: Learning to Like Our Looks and Ourselves, Rita Freeman, Ph.D.

[16] Clinebell and Clinebell, 1970.

Printed in the USA
CPSIA information can be obtained
at www.ICGtesting.com
LVHW081947111124
796318LV00005B/512